DEAN CLOSE SCHOOL

LIBRARY

This book must be returned by the latest date stamped below.

(08.04.83)

PREFACES TO SHAKESPEARE
by Harley Granville-Barker

The complete Prefaces are available in paperback format, divided into seven volumes:

Hamlet

King Lear.   Macbeth

Othello

Julius Caesar.   Antony and Cleopatra

Coriolanus

Love's Labour's Lost.   Romeo and Juliet.   The Merchant of Venice

The Winter's Tale.   Twelfth Night.   A Midsummer Night's Dream

PREFACE TO KING LEAR
© HARLEY GRANVILLE-BARKER 1930
© IN USA AND CANADA
BY PRINCETON UNIVERSITY PRESS 1946
© OUTSIDE THE USA AND CANADA
THE TRUSTEES OF THE AUTHOR 1958

FIRST PUBLISHED 1930
FIRST PUBLISHED IN THIS EDITION 1984

PREFACE TO MACBETH
© THE TRUSTEES OF THE HARLEY GRANVILLE-BARKER ESTATE 1974

FIRST PUBLISHED 1974
FIRST PUBLISHED IN THIS EDITION 1984

PRINTED IN GREAT BRITAIN
BY BIDDLES LTD, GUILDFORD, SURREY
FOR THE PUBLISHERS
B. T. BATSFORD LTD
4 FITZHARDINGE STREET, LONDON W1H 0AH

ISBN 0 7134 4512 2

FOREWORD
by Sir John Gielgud

A NUMBER of older players used to describe Harley Granville-Barker to me very vividly as he was when they had worked with him before the 1914–18 War.

He had been slim and poetic-looking in those days, a vegetarian like his close friend and mentor Bernard Shaw. Wearing sandals and chewing nuts, infinitely demanding as he was when directing Shakespeare, they strove to please him in his striving for perfection, and were lost in admiration of his innovations—an almost uncut text, only two intervals and a simple stylized decor, with a builtout forestage, no footlights, and a breakneck speed in delivery from his cast. On first nights he would pin last minute notes of exhortation on their dressing-room mirrors: 'Be swift, be swift, be not poetical' (to Cathleen Nesbitt as Perdita).

When I first caught sight of him myself in 1928 he looked impressive enough, but more like a successful businessman. He was beginning to put on weight, and wore a dark suit and a Homburg hat. But I was instantly to become aware of his sureness and authority. Even though his wife (watching jealously from the darkness of the dress circle), interrupted him once or twice with a firm 'Harley! lunch . . .' to which, alas, he obediently complied, he had contrived in two short hours to redirect (and even in one of the plays recast the leading part) with unerring and unimpeachable finality.

Though he lived for a time in England, he soon became dissatisfied with trying to become a country squire and moved to Paris. Here he wrote the Shakespeare *Prefaces* and lectured at the Sorbonne. In 1937–8, when he came to see some Shakespearean productions of mine, he wrote me a number of brilliant letters of criticism which I had the good sense to keep. And in 1939, when I was to take *Hamlet* to Elsinore, after a preliminary week at the Lyceum, I heard he was in London and wrote begging him to come to a late rehearsal. Next morning he summoned me to the Ritz, and gave me three hours of invaluable and detailed notes with which I was able to improve my own performance and that of my company.

Finally, in 1940, Lewis Casson and Tyrone Guthrie prevailed on him to help us in a production of *King Lear* at the Old Vic. He stayed at the Athenaeum and for ten days we had him to ourselves. Of those ten days of rehearsals at the Vic I have written some account elsewhere. Even the Fall of France, which was to appal us some weeks later, could not make me forget the magic excitement of working under Barker for those few short days—the agonising struggles to satisfy his demands, the devastating accuracy of his strictures, the enormous satisfaction of earning an occasional note of approval. Then, just after the first dress rehearsal, he was gone, though during the subsequent weeks he would still write me postcards mentioning points which he had reconsidered and things that he had meant to say.

In 1945 I was playing Hamlet again for the last time and heard he had been to see a matinée. Rather timidly I invited him and his wife to dine with me at my house on the very night when Peace was to be declared. But I found him considerably aged and silent and did not press him to talk about the theatre before his wife. After dinner, however, he did draw me aside and said some kind things about my performance. A few days later he wrote me a last letter, apologising for not having remembered the 1939 production and the help he had given me in improving it.

The following year he died in Paris, but though with a few of his staunchest admirers, I begged to be allowed to organise a Memorial Service, Mrs Barker sent strict injunctions that she had no wish for him to be publicly commemorated 'by actors' and we were forced to abandon the idea. I can hardly believe that Barker would have approved her decision. Though he plainly despised the commercial trappings of our profession—its gossip, intrigue and jealousy, its publicity, cheapness and ephemeral glories and disasters—I cannot but think of him as a great master, the nearest theatrical equivalent to Toscanini among the many brilliant colleagues I have been fortunate to work with during my long career.

July 1981

John Gielgud

King Lear

"LEAR is essentially impossible to be represented on a stage"—and later critics have been mostly of Charles Lamb's opinion. My chief business in this Preface will be to justify, if I can, its title there.

Shakespeare meant it to be acted, and he was a very practical playwright. So that should count for something. Acted it was, and with success enough for it to be presented before the king at Whitehall. (Whatever his faults, James I seems to have had a liking for good drama.) And Burbage's performance of King Lear remained a vivid memory. At the Restoration it was one of the nine plays selected by Davenant for his theater. He had in mind, doubtless, its "reforming and making fit"—all of them except *Hamlet* and *Othello* were to suffer heavily from that. But Downes, his prompter, tells us that it was ". . . *Acted* exactly as Mr *Shakespear* wrote it. . . . "—several times apparently—before Nahum Tate produced his version in 1681. This hotchpotch held the stage for the next hundred and fifty years and more, though from Garrick's time onwards it would generally be somewhat re-Shakespeareanized.[1] One cannot prove Shakespearean stage-worthiness by citing Tate, but how far is it not Tate rather than Shakespeare that Lamb condemns? He has Shakespeare's play in mind, but he had never seen it acted. Part of his complaint is that ". . . Tate has put his hook in the nostrils of this Leviathan, for Garrick and his followers, the showmen of the scene, to draw the mighty beast about more easily." And he never considers Shakespeare's play in relation to Shakespeare's stage. He came near to doing so; for, later in the essay, with *The Tempest* for

---

[1] Elliston and Kean, after a little hesitation, went so far as to restore the tragic ending. Then, in 1838, Macready acted Shakespeare's play again. But even he tampered with its structure, and—by much omission—with its text.

theme, he speaks of ". . . the elaborate and anxious provision of
scenery, which the luxury of the age demands . . ." which ". . .
works a quite contrary effect to what is intended. That which in
comedy, or plays of familiar life, adds so much to the life of the
imitation, in plays which appeal to the higher faculties positively
destroys the illusion which it is introduced to aid." Had he followed out this argument with *King Lear* for an example, giving
credit to Shakespeare the playwright as well as to Shakespeare the
poet—I do not say that he would have reached a different conclu-
sion, for there is still the plea to be met that here, for once, Shakespeare the playwright did overreach himself, but he must at least
have recognized another side to the question. Lamb's essay should
be read, of course, as a whole. He loved the drama; the theater
alternately delighted and exasperated him. The orotund acting of
his day, its conventional tricks, can have been but a continual
offense to his sensitive ear and nicety of taste. He here takes his
revenge—and it is an ample one—for many evenings of such
suffering. He never stopped to consider whether there might not
be more even to the actor's despised art than that.

A profounder and a more searching indictment of the play's
stage-worthiness comes from A. C. Bradley in the (for me) most
remarkable of those remarkable lectures on Shakespearean Tragedy. To him it seems ". . . Shakespeare's greatest achievement, but
. . . *not* his best play." The entire argument should be read; but
this, I think, sums it up not unfairly. He says that "The stage is
the test of strictly dramatic quality, and *King Lear* is too huge for
the stage. . . . It has scenes immensely effective in the theatre;
three of them—the two between Lear and Goneril and between
Lear, Goneril and Regan, and the ineffably beautiful scene in the
Fourth Act between Lear and Cordelia—lose in the theatre very
little of the spell they have for imagination; and the gradual inter-
weaving of the two plots is almost as masterly as in *Much Ado*. But
(not to speak of defects due to mere carelessness) that which
makes the *peculiar* greatness of *King Lear*,—the immense scope
of the work; the mass and variety of intense experience which it
contains; the interpenetration of sublime imagination, piercing
pathos, and humour almost as moving as the pathos; the vastness
of the convulsion both of nature and of human passion; the vagueness of the scene where the action takes place, and of the move-

ments of the figures which cross this scene; the strange atmosphere, cold and dark, which strikes on us as we enter this scene, enfolding those figures and magnifying their dim outlines like a winter mist; the half-realised suggestions of vast universal powers working in the world of individual fears and passions, all this interferes with dramatic clearness even when the play is read, and in the theatre not only refuses to reveal itself fully through the sense but seems to be almost in contradiction with their reports." And later: "The temptation of Othello and the scene of Duncan's murder may lose upon the stage, but they do not lose their *essence*, and they gain as well as lose. The Storm-scenes in *King Lear* gain nothing, and their very *essence* is destroyed." For this essence is poetry, and, he concludes, ". . . such poetry as cannot be transferred to the space behind the foot-lights, but has its being only in imagination. Here then is Shakespeare at his very greatest, but not the mere dramatist Shakespeare."

Notice, first of all, how widely Bradley's standpoint is removed from that—we may venture to surmise it—of "the mere dramatist Shakespeare" and his fellows the actors. To say of certain scenes that they were "immensely effective in the theatre" and add that they *lost* there "very little of the spell they have for imagination," to argue that "the temptation of Othello and the scene of Duncan's murder may lose upon the stage, but they do not lose their *essence*, and they gain as well as lose"—it would have sounded to them queer commendation. For in whatever Shakespeare wrote was the implied promise that in the theater it would *gain*. Bradley passes easily to: "The Storm-scenes in *King Lear* gain nothing, and their very *essence* is destroyed." But the dramatist, on his defense, would rightly refuse to follow him; for the premises to the argument are not the same.

Bradley and Lamb may be right in their conclusions. It is possible that this most practical and loyal of dramatists did for once —despite himself, driven to it by his unpremeditating genius— break his promise and betray his trust by presenting to his fellows a play, the capital parts of which they simply could not act. Happily for them, they and their audiences never found him out. But if Bradley is right, not the most perfect performance can be a fulfillment, can be aught but a betrayal of *King Lear*. There is the issue. The thing is, of course, incapable of proof. The best that imperfect human actors can give must come short of perfection, and the critic can always retort to their best that his imagination betters it. Bradley's argument is weighty. Yet—with all deference to a great critic—I protest that, as it stands, it is not valid. He is contending that a practical and practiced dramatist has here written a largely impracticable play. Before condemning these "Storm-scenes" he should surely consider their stagecraft—their mere stagecraft. For may not "the mere dramatist" have his answer hidden there? But this—starting from his standpoint of imaginative reader—he quite neglects to do.

Ought we, moreover, to assume—as Bradley seems to—that a play must necessarily make all its points and its full effect, point by point, clearly and completely, scene by scene, as the performance goes along? Not every play, I think. For the appreciation of such a work as *King Lear* one might even demand the second or third hearing of the whole, which the alertest critic would need to give to (say) a piece of music of like caliber. But leave that aside. No condoning of an ultimate obscurity is involved. And comedy, it can be admitted, demands an immediate clarity. Nor is the dramatist ever to be dispensed from making his story currently clear and at least provisionally significant. But he has so much more than that to do. He must produce a constant illusion of life. To do this he must, among other things, win us to something of a fellow-feeling with his characters; and even, at the play's critical moments, to identifying their emotions with our own.

Now the *significance* of their emotions may well not be clear to the characters themselves for the moment, their only certainty be of the intensity of the emotions themselves. There are devices enough by which, if the dramatist wishes, this significance can be kept currently clear to the audience. There is the Greek chorus; the earlier Elizabethans turned Prologue and Presenters to account; the *raisonneur* of nineteenth century comedy has a respectable ancestry. Shakespeare uses the *raisonneur* in varying guises. In this very play we detect him in the Fool, and in Edgar turned Poor Tom. But note that both they and their "reasoning" are blended not only into the action but into the moral scheme, and are never allowed to lower its emotional temperature by didactics —indeed they stimulate it. For here will be the difficulty in preserving that "dramatic clearness" which Bradley demands; it would cost—and repeatedly be costing—dramatist and actors their emotional, their illusionary, hold upon their audience. Lear's progress dramatic and spiritual lies through a dissipation of egoism; submission to the cruelty of an indifferent Nature, less cruel to him than are his own kin; to ultimate loss of himself in madness. Consider the effect of this—of the battling of storm without and storm within, of the final breaking of that Titan spirit—if Shakespeare merely let us look on, critically observant. From such a standpoint, Lear is an intolerable tyrant, and Regan and Goneril have a case against him. We should not side with them; but our onlooker's sympathy might hardly be warmer than, say, the kindly Albany's.[2] And Shakespeare needs to give us more than sympathy with Lear, and something deeper than understanding. If the verity of his ordeal is really to be brought home to us, we must, in as full a sense as may be, pass through it with him, must make the experience and its overwhelming emotions momentarily our own.

Shakespeare may (it can be argued) have set himself an impossible task; but if he is to succeed it will only be by these means. In this mid-crisis of the play he must never relax his emotional hold on us. And all these things of which Bradley complains, the confusion of pathos, humor and sublime imagination, the vastness of the convulsion, the vagueness of the scene and the movements of the characters, the strange atmosphere and the half-realized suggestions—all this he needs as material for Lear's experience, and ours. Personally, I do not find quite so much vagueness and confusion. To whatever metaphysical heights Lear himself may rise, some character (Kent and Gloucester through the storm and in the hovel, Edgar for the meeting with the blinded Gloucester), some circumstance, or a few salient and explicit phrases will always be found pointing the action on its way. And if we become so at one with Lear in his agony that for the time its full significance escapes us, may not memory still make this clear? For that is very often true of our own emotional experiences. We are in confusion of suffering or joy at the time; only later do we realize, as we say, "what it all meant to us." It is, I suggest, this natural

---

[2] Whom Shakespeare carefully keeps out of the angry scenes which lead to Lear's self-banishment to the wild and the storm.

bent which Shakespeare turns to his account in these larger passages of *King Lear*. In the acting they move us profoundly. The impression they make remains. And when the play is over they, with the rest of it, should cohere in the memory, and clarify; and the meaning of the whole should be plain. Shakespeare, I protest, has not failed; he has—to the degree of his endeavor—triumphantly succeeded. But to appreciate the success and give effect to it in the play's performance we must master and conform to the stagecraft on which it depends.

In this hardest of tasks—the showing of Lear's agony, his spiritual death and resurrection—we find Shakespeare relying very naturally upon his strongest weapon, which by experiment and practice he has now, indeed, forged to an extraordinary strength, and to a suppleness besides: the weapon of dramatic poetry. He has, truly, few others of any account. In the storm-scenes the shaking of a thunder-sheet will not greatly stir us. A modern playwright might seek help in music—but the music of Shakespeare's day is not of that sort; in impressive scenery—he has none. He has, in compensation, the fluidity of movement which the negative background of his stage allows him. For the rest, he has his actors, their acting and the power of their speech. It is not a mere rhetorical power, nor are the characters lifted from the commonplace simply by being given verse to speak instead of conversational prose. All method of expression apart, they are *poetically conceived*; they exist in those dimensions, in that freedom, and are endowed with that peculiar power. They are dramatic poetry incarnate.

Thus it is that Shakespeare can make such calls upon them as here he must. In the storm-scenes they not only carry forward the story, revealing and developing themselves as they do so, they must—in default of other means—create the storm besides. Not by detachedly describing it; if they "lose themselves" in its description, they will for that while lose something of their own hold on us. The storm is not in itself, moreover, dramatically important, only in its effect upon Lear. How, then, to give it enough magnificence to impress him, yet keep it from rivaling him? Why, by identifying the storm with him, setting the actor to impersonate both Lear and—reflected in Lear—the storm. That, approximately, is the effect made when—the Fool cowering,

drenched and pitiful, at his side—he launches into the tre-
mendous:

> Blow, winds, and crack your cheeks! rage! blow!
> You cataracts and hurricanoes, spout
> Till you have drench'd our steeples, drown'd the cocks!
> You sulphurous and thought-executing fires,
> Vaunt-couriers of oak-cleaving thunder-bolts,
> Singe my white head! And thou, all-shaking thunder,
> Strike flat the thick rotundity of the world!
> Crack nature's moulds, all germens spill at once
> That make ungrateful man.

This is no mere description of a storm, but in music and imaginative suggestion a dramatic creating of the storm itself; and
there is Lear—and here are we, if we yield ourselves—in the
midst of it, almost a part of it. Yet Lear himself, in his Promethean
defiance, still dominates the scene.

But clearly the effect cannot be made by Lamb's "old man
tottering about the stage with a walking-stick"; and by any such
competitive machinery for thunder and lightning as Bradley quite
needlessly assumes to be an inevitable part of the play's staging it
will be largely spoiled. What actor in his senses, however, would
attempt to act the scene "realistically"? (I much doubt if any one
of Lamb's detested barnstormers ever did.) And as to the thunder
and lightning, Shakespeare uses the modicum to his hand; but it
is of no dramatic consequence, and his stagecraft takes no account
of it.[8] Yet if the human Lear seems lost for a moment in the symbolic figure, here is the Fool to remind us of him:

> O nuncle, court holy water in a dry house is better than this
> rain-water out o' door. Good nuncle, in, ask thy daughters' bless-
> ing; here's a night pities neither wise men nor fools.

—and to keep the scene in touch with reality. Yet note that the
fantasy of the Fool only *mitigates* the contrast, and the spell is
held unbroken. It is not till later—when Lear's defiant rage, hav-

---

[8] Bradley argues in a footnote that *because* Shakespeare's "means of imitating
a storm were so greatly inferior to ours" he could not have "had the stage-
performance only or chiefly in view in composing these scenes." But this is,
surely, to view Shakespeare's theater and its craft with modern eyes. The contem-
porary critic would have found it easier to agree that just *because* your imitation
storm was such a poor affair you must somehow make your stage effect *without*
relying on it.

ing painted us the raging of the storm, has subsided—that Kent's sound, most "realistic" common sense, persuading him to the shelter of the hovel, is admitted.

But Shakespeare has other means of keeping the human and the apocalyptic Lear at one. Though the storm is being painted for us still—

> Rumble thy bellyfull spit, fire! spout, rain!
> Nor rain, wind, thunder, fire are my daughters:
> I tax not you, you elements, with unkindness;
> I never gave you kingdom, call'd you children,
> You owe me no subscription: then let fall
> Your horrible pleasure; here I stand, your slave;
> A poor, infirm, weak and despis'd old man.

—both in the sense of the words and the easier cadence of the verse the human Lear is emerging, and emerges fully upon the sudden simplicity of

> here I stand, your slave;
> A poor, infirm, weak and despis'd old man.

But the actor is not meant, therefore, suddenly to drop from trenchant speech to commonplace, present us a pathological likeness of poverty, infirmity and the rest, divest himself of all poetic power, become, in fact, the old man with a walking-stick. For if he does he will incontinently and quite fatally cease to be the Lear that Shakespeare has, as we said, conceived and embodied in poetry. In poetry; not, one must again insist, necessarily or simply in verse. And it is no more, now or later, a mere question of a method of speaking than of form in the writing. Verse, prose, and doggerel rhyme, in those strenuous scenes, each has its use, each asks an appropriate beauty of treatment, and the three in harmony are, by dramatic title, poetry.

The actor has then, not simply or chiefly to speak poetically, but, for the while, somehow to incarnate this poetry in himself. He can do so—paradoxically—by virtue of an exceptional self-sacrifice. Physically, Shakespeare's Lear must surrender to *him*; he makes himself in return an intellectual and emotional instrument for its expression. That is the way of all honest acting. If the actor's personality is the richer, a character will be absorbed in it. In a play of familiar human commerce actor and character may collaborate, so to say, upon equal terms. But give the character the transcendent quality of poetry, the actor can no longer bring it within the realistic limits of his personality. He may—obtusely —try to decompose it into a realism of impersonation, decorated by "poetic" speech. It is such a treatment of Lear which produces Lamb's old man with a walking-stick, and, for Bradley, dissipates the poetic atmosphere. But what Shakespeare asks of his actor is to surrender as much of himself as he can—much must remain; all that is physical—to this metaphysical power.

The thing is easier to do than to analyze. Children, set to act Shakespeare, will fling themselves innocently at the greatest of the plays; and, just because they do not comprehend and so cannot subdue the characters to their own likeness, they let us see them—though diminished and feeble—as through a clear glass. For the matured actor it is not quite so easy. He must comprehend the character, identify himself with it, and then—forget himself in it. Yet in this play and these very scenes he will find the example of Lear's own relation to the storm; in the reflection of its grandeur upon him, and the force lent by his fellowship with it to the storm devouring his mind. One must not push the comparison too far, nor is the psychology of acting a subject to be compassed in a sentence or two. But very much as the storm's strength is added to Lear's when he abandons himself to its apprehension, so may the Lear of Shakespeare's poetic and dramatic art be embodied in the actor if he will but do the same. And *there* should be the Lear of Lamb's demand, great "not in corporal dimension but in intellectual." Upon a "realistic" stage the thing cannot well be done. With Shakespeare made to delegate half his privileges to scene-painter and property-man a like dissociation will be forced upon the actor. And it is not only that the apparently real heath and hovel and the all but real thunder and lightning will reduce the characters which move among them to mere matter of fact also, but that by the dissociation itself, the appeal to our imagination—upon which all depends—is compromised. For the strength of this lies in its unity and concentration. It is the unity of the appeal that allows Shakespeare to bring so much within its scope. And, with time, place and circumstance, night, storm and desolation, and man's capacity to match them in despair all caught into a few lines of poetry, it should not be so hard to absorb besides—he willing—the ego of the actor who speaks them.

Then he will stand before us not physically ridiculous by comparison with them, but invested with their dynamic quality.

Shakespeare contrives within this harmony the full range of the effects he needs. There are not two Lears—the Titan integrating the storm and the old man breaking under it. In the accommodating realm of dramatic poetry they can remain one. Those contrasted aspects of them are shown in the swift descent we noted from magniloquence to simplicity, from rivalry with the elements to the confession of

> here I stand, your slave;
> A poor, infirm, weak and despis'd old man.

Or, we may say, there are the two Lears in one: the old man pathetic by contrast with the elements, yet terribly great in our immediate sense of his identity with them.

At best, of course, the actor can be but a token of the ideal Lear; and (thanking him) some of us may still feel that in the rarefied spaces of our imagination without his aid we come nearer to Shakespeare's imaginings—though what have we after all but a token of words upon paper to measure these by? But does the actor only remove us a stage farther from our source? I think not. He gives the words objectivity and life. Shakespeare has provided for his intervention. He can at least be a true token.

The Main Lines of Construction

King Lear, alone among the great tragedies, adds to its plot a subplot fully developed. And it suffers somewhat under the burden. After a few preliminary lines—Shakespeare had come to prefer this to the grand opening, and in this instance they are made introductory to plot and subplot too—we have a full and almost formal statement of the play's main theme and a show of the characters that are to develop it, followed by a scene which sets out the subplot as fully. The two scenes together form a sort of double dramatic prologue; and they might, by modern custom, count as a first act, for after them falls the only clearly indicated time-division in the play. The Folio, however, adds the quarrel with Goneril before an act-pause is allowed: then—whatever its authority, but according to its usual plan—sets out four more acts, the second allotted to the parallel quarrel with Regan, the third to the climax of the main theme; the fourth we may call a picture of the wreck of both Lear and Gloucester, and in it sub-plot and main plot are blended, and the fifth act is given to the final and rather complex catastrophe. This division, then, has thus much dramatic validity, and a producer may legitimately choose to abide by it. On the other hand, one may contend, the play's action flows unchecked throughout (but for the one check which does not coincide with the act-division of the Folio). Still it is not to be supposed that a Jacobean audience did, or a modern audience would, sit through a performance without pause. Yet again, it does not follow that the Folio's act-divisions were ob-served as intervals in which the audience dispersed and by which the continuity of dramatic effect was altogether broken. A pro-ducer must, I think, exercise his own judgment. There may be something to be said for more "breathing-spaces," but I should myself incline to one definite interval only, to fall after Act III. To this point the play is carried by one great impetus of inspira-tion, and there will be great gain in its acting being as unchecked. If the strain on actors or audience seems to be too great, I should choose a breathing-space after Act I, Scene ii, for all the Folio's authority to the contrary. But the strain should not be excessive upon either audience or actors. Shakespeare's stagecraft—his inter-weaving of contrasted characters and scenes—provides against this, as does the unity of impression and rapidity of action, which his unlocalized staging makes possible.[4]

The scene in which Lear divides his kingdom s a magnificent statement of a magnificent theme. It has a proper formality, and there is a certain megalithic grandeur about it, Lear dominating it, that we associate with Greek tragedy. Its probabilities are neither here nor there. A dramatist may postulate any situation

[4] Modern scenic productions, even at their simplest, not only destroy this unity of impression, but lengthen the performance of the plays considerably, and the acting habits they have engendered lengthen them still more. Mr. Nugent Monck has produced *King Lear* at the Maddermarket Theatre, Norwich, upon an unlocal-ized stage. He cut approximately 750 of the 3340 lines of text (the Folio will give authority for the cutting of some 200), allowed a ten minutes' interval, did not play overrapidly, and the whole performance only lasted two hours and a half.

he has the means to interpret, if he will abide by the logic of it after. The producer should observe and even see stressed the scene's characteristics; Lear's two or three passages of such an eloquence as we rather expect at a play's climax than its opening, the strength of such single lines as

> The bow is bent and drawn, make from the shaft.

with its hammering monosyllables; and the hard-bitten

> Nothing: I have sworn; I am firm.

together with the loosening of the tension in changes to rhymed couplets, and the final drop into prose by that businesslike couple, Goneril and Regan. Then follows, with a lift into lively verse for a start, as a contrast and as the right medium for Edmund's sanguine conceit, the development of the Gloucester theme. Shakespeare does this at his ease, allows himself diversion and time. He has now both the plot of the ungrateful daughters and the subplot of the treacherous son under way.

But the phenomenon for which Shakespeareans learn to look has not yet occurred, that inexplicable "springing to life"—a springing, it almost seems, into a life of its own—of character or theme. Very soon it does occur; Lear's entrance, disburdened from the care of state, is its natural signal. On his throne, rightly enough, he showed formal and self-contained. Now he springs away; and now the whole play in its relation to him takes on a liveliness and variety; nor will the energy be checked or weakened, or, if checked, only that the next stroke may be intenser, till the climax is past, till his riven and exhausted nature is granted the oblivion of sleep. This is the master-movement of the play, which enshrines the very soul of the play—and in the acting, as I have suggested, there should be no break allowed. To read and give full imaginative value to those fifteen hundred lines at a stretch is certainly exhausting; if they were written at one stretch of inspiration the marvel is that Shakespeare, with his Lear, did not collapse under the strain, yet the exactions of his performance he tempers with all his skill. Lear is surrounded by characters, which each in a different way take a share of the burden from him. Kent, the Fool, and Edgar as Poor Tom are a complement of dramatic strength; and the interweaving of the scenes con-

cerning Oswald, Edmund and Gloucester saves the actor's energy
for the scenes of the rejection and the storm.[5]

As the Lear theme expanded under his hand Shakespeare had
begun, and perforce, to economize his treatment of the Gloucester-
Edgar-Edmund story. Edgar himself is indeed dismissed from
the second scene upon no more allowance of speech than

> I'm sure on't, not a word.

—with which the best of actors may find it hard to make his
presence felt; and at our one view of him before he had been left
negative enough. Edmund is then brought rapidly into relation
with the main plot, and the blending of main plot and subplot
begins.[6] Edgar also is drawn into Lear's orbit; and, for the time,

---

[5] Therefore the producer who will for the sake of his scenery (as has been the
pleasant picture-stage custom) run two or three of the storm-scenes into one,
presents himself and his Lear with failure.

[6] We find, too, at this point, some signs that the emphasis of the play's whole
scheme was altered.

> Have you heard of no likely wars toward,
> 'Twixt the Dukes of Cornwall and Albany?

Curan asks Edmund, who answers "Not a word." Edmund, with admirable
promptitude, turns the notion to the further confusing of the so easily confused
Edgar, but the wars themselves come to nothing. Kent, in an involved speech in
Act III (for him most uncharacteristically involved), suggests that it is the threat
of them which is bringing the French army to England. But the vagueness is
suspicious. It looks a little as if Shakespeare had thought of making the hypocrite
inheritors of Cordelia's portion fall out over it (an obvious nemesis) and had
changed his mind. There are slight signs indeed that greed of possessions was to
have been the axis for the whole play to turn upon. It begins with the parting
of the realm; and

> Legitimate Edgar, I must have your land. . . .

is the coping point of Edmund's first soliloquy. Did the discovery of deeper spiritual issues in Lear's own character and fate give us the present play? Another and
a later change in the plot can be divined. The King of France comes armed with
Cordelia to Lear's rescue, as is natural. Then, by virtue of the clumsiest few lines
in the play, he is sent back again. Did Shakespeare originally mean Cordelia to
restore her father to his throne as in the old play; but would a French victory in
England not have done? It may be; though I cannot think he ever intended Lear
to survive. On the other hand, Cordelia herself is not a figure predoomed to death.
This catastrophe, though the moral violence of the play may aesthetically justify
it, and though it is needed dramatically, as a final blow to Lear (see p. 45 for
the fuller argument of this), always seems to me a wrench from his first plan.
This decided on, though, he would certainly have to get rid of France. The point
for the producer is that the Folio cuts the clumsy explanation, as if on the principle—and it is an excellent one in the theater—of: "Never explain, never apologize."
In fact it cuts the whole scene, which later contains as dramatically feeble an excuse

to the complete sacrifice of his own interests in the play. "Poor Tom" is in effect an embodiment of Lear's frenzy, the disguise no part of Edgar's own development.

As we have seen, while Act III is at the height of its argument, Shakespeare is careful to keep alive the lower-pitched theme of Edmund's treachery, his new turn to the betrayal of his father He affords it two scenes, of twenty-five lines each, wedged between the three dominant scenes of the storm and Lear's refuge from it. They are sufficient and no more for their own purpose; in their sordidness they stand as valuable contrast to the spiritual exaltation of the others. The supreme moment for Lear himself. the turning point, therefore, of the play's main theme, is reached in the second of the three storm-scenes, when the proud old king kneels humbly and alone in his wretchedness to pray. This is the argument's absolute height; and from now on we may feel (as far as Lear is concerned) the tension relax, through the first grim passage of his madness, slackening still through the fantastic scene of the arraignment of the joint-stools before that queer bench of justices, to the moment of his falling asleep and his conveyance away—his conveyance, we find it to be, out of the main stream of the play's action. Shakespeare then deals the dreadful blow to Gloucester. The very violence and horror of this finds its dramatic justification in the need to match in another sort—since he could not hope to match it in spiritual intensity—the catastrophe to Lear. And now we may imagine him, if we please, stopping to consider where he was. Anticlimax, after this, is all but inevitable. Let the producer take careful note how Shakespeare sets out to avoid the worst dangers of it.[7]

for the delay in handing Lear over to his daughter's care, though it gives none for the devoted Kent letting the distracted old man out of his sight to roam the fields crowned with wild flowers. I think on the whole that the Folio gives a producer a good lead. Yet another slight change of plan may be guessed at; it would effect some economy in the working-out of the subplot. Edmund says to Gloucester about Edgar:

If your honour judge it meet, I will place you where you shall hear us confer of this . . . and that without any further delay than this very evening.

But he never does. Shakespeare may have remembered, besides, that he had lately used this none too fresh device in *Othello*.

[7] It is worth remarking here upon the fact that of Edgar's two soliloquies—the one which ends Act III, Scene vi, and the one which begins Act IV—the Folio omits the first. They are somewhat redundant in mood if not in matter. The interesting thing is that the Folio omission is of a speech ending a scene and

Had the play been written upon the single subject of Lear and his daughters, we should now be in sight of its end. But the wealth of material Shakespeare has posited asks for use, and his own imagination, we may suppose, is still teeming. But by the very nature of the material (save Cordelia) left for development the rest of the play must be pitched in a lower key. Shakespeare marshals the action by which the wheel of Gloucester's weakness and Edmund's treachery is brought full circle with extraordinary skill and even more extraordinary economy. Yet for all this, except in a fine flash or two, the thing stays by comparison pedestrian. He is only on the wing again when Lear and Cordelia are his concern; in the scenes of their reconciliation and of the detached tragedy of Lear's death with the dead Cordelia in his arms, as in the still more detached and—as far as the mere march of the action is concerned—wholly unjustifiable scene of Lear mad and fantastically crowned with wild flowers. We must add, though, to the inspired passages the immediately preceding fantasy of Gloucester's imaginary suicide, an apt offset to the realistic horror of his blinding, and occasion for some inimitable verse. The chief fact to face, then, is that for the rest of the play, the best will be incidental and not a necessary part of the story.[8] The producer therefore must give his own best attention to Albany, Goneril and Regan and their close-packed contests, and to the nice means by which Edgar is shaped into a hero; and in general must see that this purposeful disciplined necessary stuff is given fullness and, as far as may be, spontaneity of life in its interpretation. If he will take care of this the marvelous moments will tend to take care of him.

Shakespeare strengthens the action at once with the fresh interest of the Edmund-Goneril-Regan intrigue, daring as it is to launch into this with the short time left him for its development and resolving. He is, indeed, driven to heroic compressions, to impli-

---

moralizing upon the event; it forms a "considering point." Without it the catastrophe to Gloucester is linked more closely to Lear's misfortunes, and the long due development of Edgar's character then begins—and importantly—the fourth act. For further argument upon this point, see pp. 65, 77.

[8] The meeting of mad Lear and blind Gloucester (I give the scene more attention on p. 41) is, of course, most germane to the play's *idea*—a more important thing to Shakespeare than the mere story—but it does check the march of the story.

cations, effects by "business," action "off," almost to "love-making by reference only." Goneril's first approach to Edmund (or his to her; but we may credit the lady, I think, with the throwing of the handkerchief) is only clearly marked out for the actors by Regan's reference to it five scenes later, when she tells us that at Goneril's

> late being here
> She gave strange œilliads and most speaking looks
> To noble Edmund.

(Regan credits her with what, if we prefer our Shakespeare modernized, we might literally translate into "giving the glad eye.") But this silent business of the earlier scene is important and must be duly marked if the arrival of the two together and Edmund's turning back to avoid meeting Albany, the "mild husband," is to have its full effect. For the first and last of their spoken love-making, excellently characteristic as it is, consists of Goneril's

> Our wishes on the way
> May prove effects. . . .
> This trusty servant
> Shall pass between us: ere long you are like to hear,
> If you dare venture in your own behalf,
> A mistress's command. Wear this; spare speech;
> Decline your head: this kiss, if it durst speak,
> Would stretch thy spirits up into the air.
> Conceive, and fare thee well.

and Edmund's ("Spare speech," indeed!)

> Yours in the ranks of death!

—all spoken in Oswald's presence too. It is, of course, not only excellent but sufficient. The regal impudency of the woman, the falsely chivalrous flourish of the man's response—pages of dialogue might not tell us more of their relations; and, of these relations, is there much more that is dramatically worth knowing? The point for the producer is that no jot of such a constricted dramatic opportunity must be missed.

For the whole working-out of this lower issue of the play the same warning stands true; an exact and unblurred value must be given to each significant thing. The interaction of circumstance and character is close-knit and complex, but it is clear. Keep it clear and it can be made effective to any audience that will listen, and is not distracted from listening. Let us underline this last phrase and now make the warning twofold. In working out a theme so full of incident and of contending characters Shakespeare allows for no distraction of attention at all, certainly not for the breaking of continuity which the constant shifting of realistically localized scenery must involve. The action, moreover, of these later scenes is exceptionally dependent upon to-ings and fro-ings. Given continuity of performance and no more insistence upon whereabouts than the action itself will indicate, the impression produced by the constant busy movement into our sight and out again of purposeful, passionate or distracted figures, is in itself of great dramatic value, and most congruous to the plot and counter-plot of the play's ending. The order for Lear's and Cordelia's murder, the quarrel over Edmund's precedence, Albany's sudden self-assertion, Regan's sickness, Edgar's appearance, the fight, his discovery of himself, Goneril's discomfiture, the telling of Kent's secret, Regan's and Goneril's death, the alarm to save Lear and Cordelia—Shakespeare, by the Folio text, gets all this into less than two hundred lines, with a fair amount of rhetoric and inci-dental narrative besides. He needs no more, though bareness does nearly turn to banality sometimes. But unless we can be held in an unrelaxed grip we may not submit to the spell.

He has kept a technical master-stroke for his ending:

Enter Lear with Cordelia in his arms.

There should be a long, still pause, while Lear passes slowly in with his burden, while they all stand respectful as of old to his majesty. We may have wondered a little that Shakespeare should be content to let Cordelia pass from the play as casually as she seems to in the earlier scene. But this is the last of her, not that. Dumb and dead, she that was never apt of speech—what fitter finish for her could there be? What fitter ending to the history of the two of them, which began for us with Lear on his throne, conscious of all eyes on him, while she shamed and angered him by her silence? The same company are here, or all but the same, and they await his pleasure.[9] Even Regan and Goneril are here to

---

[9] And this must not be counted as chance, for the bodies of Goneril and Regan have been brought on—why else?

pay him a ghastly homage. But he knows none of them—save for a blurred moment Kent whom he banished—none but Cordelia. And again he reproaches her silence; for

> Her voice was ever soft,
> Gentle and low, an excellent thing in woman.

Then his heart breaks.

The Method of the Dialogue

THE dialogue of *King Lear* is remarkable for its combination of freedom and power. Of the plays that neighbor it, the sustained melodies of *Othello* may give greater dignity. In *Macbeth* there are passages that seem to wield a sort of secret sway. *Antony and Cleopatra* has ease and breadth for its normal virtues as *Coriolanus* has strength; and, thereafter, Shakespeare passes to his last period of varied and delightful ease. But the exact combination of qualities that distinguishes the writing of *King Lear* we do not find again; nor indeed should we look to, since it is the product of the matter and the nature of the play. Shakespeare was in nothing a truer artist than in this, that, having mastered his means of expression, journeyed from the rhymed couplets and fantastic prose of *Love's Labour's Lost* to the perfected verse and balanced prose of *Henry V* and the mature Comedies, he yet fettered himself in no fixed style. He may write carelessly; here and there amid the poetic splendors we find what seem to be claptrap couplets and lines flatter than a pancake. But, his imagination once fired, the idea seldom fails of the living vesture it needs. This, it may be said, it is any writer's business to discover. But Shakespeare's art lies in the resource, which can give individual expression to a thought or emotion within the bounds, for instance, of a stretch of formal verse if his first need is for the solid strength of this; or, more often, in the molding of verse and prose into such variety of expressive form that it is a wonder any unity of effect is kept at all—yet it is. It lies in the daring by which, for a scene or two, he may dispense with all unity of form whatever, if his dramatic purpose will so profit. Witness such a seemingly haphazard mixture of verse, prose and snatches of song as we find in the scenes between Lear, Kent, Gloucester, the Fool and Poor Tom. Yet the dramatic vitality of these scenes lies largely in this variety and balance of orchestration; their emotional strain might be intolerable without it. But the root of the matter, of course, is in the imaginative vitality with which he dowers the characters themselves. It is always instructive to watch Shakespeare getting his play with its crew under way, to see him stating his subjects, setting his characters in opposition. Some lead off, fully themselves from the start, some seem to hang on his hands, saying what they have to say in sound conventional phrase, some he may leave all but mute, uncertain yet, it would seem, of his own use for them. Not till the whole organism has gathered strength and abounds in a life of its own is the true mastery to be seen. Even so, in *King Lear* there is more to be accounted for. In no other of the plays, I hink, unless it be *Macbeth*, are we so conscious of the force of an emotion overriding, often, a character's self-expression, and of a vision of things to which the action itself is but a foreground. And how this and the rest of the play's individuality is made manifest by the form as well as the substance of the dialogue, by the shaping and color of its verse and prose, it is, of course, of primary importance for producer and actors to observe. There is no one correct way of speaking Shakespeare's verse and prose, for he had no one way of writing it. One way grew out of another with him. Little of the method of *Romeo and Juliet* will be left in *King Lear*, much of the method of *Hamlet* still may be. But the fresh matter of a play will provoke a fresh manner, and its interpretation must be as freshly approached.

For more reasons and in more directions than one, Shakespeare seeks strength in simplicity in the writing of *King Lear*. The noble conventional speech of its beginning will not serve him long, for this is the language of such an authority as Lear discards. There is needed an expression of those fiercer, cruder strengths which come into play when a reign of order ends and a moral code is broken. Edmund begins glibly, but is indulged neither with subtle thought nor fine phrases. Goneril becomes like a woman with a fever in her: "I'll not endure it . . . I will not speak with him . . . the fault of it I'll answer . . . I'd have it come to question . . . I would breed from hence occasions, and I shall. . . ." Mark how broken is the eloquence of Lear's appeal to Regan; mark the distraction of his

> No, you unnatural hags,
> I will have such revenges on you both
> That all the world shall—I will do such things,
> What they are yet I know not, but they shall be
> The terrors of the earth. You think I'll weep;
> No, I'll not weep:
> I have full cause of weeping, but this heart
> Shall break into a hundred thousand flaws
> Or ere I'll weep.

Here, one would say, is verse reduced to its very elements.

Shakespeare has, besides, to carry us into strange regions of thought and passion, so he must, at the same time, hold us by familiar things. Lear, betrayed and helpless, at an end of his command of self or circumstance, is dramatically set above the tyranny and logic of both by being made one with the storm, and by his harmonizing with the homely fantasies of the Fool and the mad talk of Poor Tom, till his own "noble anger" breaks the bounds of reason too. Without some anchorage in simplicity, this action and these characters would range so wide that human interpretation could hardly compass them. Kent does something to keep the play's feet firm on the ground; Gloucester a little; the Fool was to Shakespeare's audience a familiar and sympathetic figure. But Lear himself might escape our closer sympathy were it not for his recurrent coming down from the heights to such moments as

> No, I will be the pattern of all patience;
> I will say nothing.

as

> My wits begin to turn.
> Come on, my boy. How dost, my boy? Art cold?
> I am cold myself. Where is this straw, my fellow?

as

> No, I will weep no more. In such a night
> To shut me out! Pour on, I will endure.
> In such a night as this!

or as

> Make no noise, make no noise; draw the curtains; so, so, so.
> We'll go to supper i' the morning; so, so, so.

This final stroke, moreover, brings us to the simplest physical actualities; Lear's defiance of the elements has flickered down to a mock pulling of the curtains round his bed. Later, when he wanders witless and alone, his speech is broken into oracular fragments of rhapsody; but the play of thought is upon actuality and his hands are at play all the time with actual things; with the flower (is it?) he takes for a coin, with whatever serves for a bit of cheese, for his gauntlet, his hat, for the challenge thrust under Gloucester's blind eyes. Let us note, too, how one of the finest passages of poetry in the play, Edgar's imaginary tale of Dover cliff, consists of the clearest-cut actualities of description. And when Lear wakes to his right senses again, simplicity is added to simplicity in his feeling the pin's prick, in his remembering not his garments. The tragic beauty of his end is made more beautiful by his call for a looking-glass, his catching at the feather to put on Cordelia's lips, the undoing of the button. These things are the necessary balance to the magniloquence of the play's beginning and to the tragic splendor of the storm.

Amid the sustained magnificence of the first scene we find the first use of an even more simple device, recurrent throughout the play.

> what can you say to draw
> A third more opulent than your sisters? Speak.
> Nothing, my lord.
> Nothing?
> Nothing.
> Nothing will come of nothing; speak again.

Again and again with varying purpose and effect Shakespeare uses this device of reiteration. Note Edmund's

> Why brand they us
> With base? with baseness? bastardy? base, base?
> . . . Well, then,
> Legitimate Edgar, I must have your land.
> Our father's love is to the bastard, Edmund,
> As to the legitimate: Fine word,—legitimate!
> Well, my legitimate, if this letter speed,
> And my invention thrive, Edmund the base
> Shall top the legitimate.

The repetition itself does much to drive in on us the insistent malice of the man.

Lear summons Oswald with

> O! you sir, you sir, come you hither, sir.
> Who am I, sir?

and the tragic counterpart of this is

> Hear, Nature, hear! dear goddess, hear.

Gloucester's grieved refrain falls casually enough:

> O, madam, my old heart is crack'd, is crack'd. . . .
> O, lady, lady, shame would have it hid. . . .
> I know not, madam; 'tis too bad, too bad.

And for a rounded elaboration of the effect, we have Lear's

> O! reason not the need; our basest beggars
> Are in the poorest thing superfluous:
> Allow not nature more than nature needs,
> Man's life is cheap as beast's. Thou art a lady;
> If only to go warm were gorgeous,
> Why, nature needs not what thou gorgeous wear'st,
> Which scarcely keeps thee warm. But, for true need—
> You heavens, give me that patience, patience I need!

Half a dozen other such instances, more or less elaborate, of major and minor importance, can be found; till we come to the effect at its crudest in

> Howl, howl, howl, howl! O, you are men of stones . . . .

and to the daring and magic of

> Thou'lt come no more.
> Never, never, never, never, never!

It is a simple device indeed, but all mature artists tend to seek strength in simplicity of expression. It is, at its simplest, a very old device, and older than drama. Iteration casts, of itself, a spell upon the listener, and the very sound of that echoing "Never" can make us sharers in Lear's helplessness and despair.[10] Bradley says of this

---

[10] It is, moreover, an old device with Shakespeare. Set beside Lear's

> O! reason not the need . . .

Juliet's

> Hath Romeo slain himself? Say thou but 'I'
> And that bare vowel 'I' shall poison more

last speech that it leaves us "on the topmost peaks of poetry"; and so, surely, it does. Rend it from its context, the claim sounds absurd; but dramatic poetry is never to be judged apart from the action it implies.

King Lear—are we still to think?—cannot be acted. The whole scheme and method of its writing is a contrivance for its effective acting. This contrast and reconciliation of grandeur and simplicity, this setting of vision in terms of actuality, this inarticulate passion which breaks now and again into memorable phrases—does not even the seeming failure of expression give us a sense of the helplessness of humanity pitted against higher powers? All the magnificent art of this is directed to one end; the play's acting in a theater.

The Characters and Their Interplay

LEAR

LEAR himself is so dominant a figure that the exhaustion of his impetus to action with the play's end barely in sight leaves Shakespeare a heavy task in the rallying of its forces for what is still to do. The argument has been raised by then, moreover, to such imaginative heights that any descent from them—even Lear's own —must be precarious. They are heights that Shakespeare himself, perhaps, did not clearly envisage till the soaring had begun. Not that there is anything tentative in the presentation of Lear. Never was character in play, one exclaims, so fully and immediately, so imminently and overwhelmingly set forth! But in this lies the actor's first difficulty.

> Than the death-dealing eye of cockatrice.
> I am not I, if there be such an 'I,'
> Or those eyes shut that make thee answer 'I.'
> If he be slain say 'I,' or if not, no;
> Brief sounds determine of my weal or woe.

The puns may destroy its emotional value for us, though they did not for the Elizabethans. But the effect aimed at is about the same. The difference in the means to it may be made one measure of Shakespeare's development of his art. Not but that he could pun dramatically to the end. He came, however, to prefer single shots to fusillades.

With the dividing of the kingdom and Cordelia's rejection the trend of the action is clearly foreshadowed:

> So be my grave my peace, as here I give
> Her father's heart from her!

By all the rules of drama we know within a little what the retribution for that must amount to; and Shakespeare will not disappoint us. But equally it would seem that for this massive fortress of pride which calls itself Lear, for any old man indeed of eighty and upwards, there could be no dramatic course but declension. Who would ever think of developing, of expanding, a character from such overwhelming beginnings? Yet this is what Shakespeare does, and finds a transcendent way to do it. So the actor's difficulty is that he must start upon a top note, at what must be pretty well the full physical stretch of his powers, yet have in reserve the means to a greater climax of another sort altogether. It is here, however, that the almost ritual formality of the first scene will help him. The occasion itself, the general subservience to Lear's tyranny (Kent's protest and Cordelia's resolution only emphasize this), Lear's own assertion of kingship as something not far from godhead, all combine to set him so above and apart from the rest that the very isolation will seem strength if the actor takes care to sustain it. There need be, there must be, no descent to petulance. Lear marking the map with his finger might be marking the land itself, so Olympian should he appear. The oath by the sacred radiance of the sun is one that only he may swear. That Kent should call him an "old man" is in itself a blasphemous outrage.

> Come not between the dragon and his wrath. . . .
>
> The bow is bent and drawn, make from the shaft. . . .
>
> Nothing: I have sworn; I am firm.

Lines like these mark the level of Lear, though their fatality may be a trifle mitigated by the human surliness of

> Better thou
> Had'st not been born than not to have pleased me better.

by the grim humor which lies in

> Nothing will come of nothing: speak again.

in the ironic last fling at Kent of

> Away! By Jupiter,
> *This* shall not be revoked.

and in the bitter gibe to Burgundy:

> When she was dear to us we did hold her so,
> But now her price is fall'n . . . .

even, one would like to suspect, in the reason given for his fast
intent to shake all cares of state from him, that he may

> Unburden'd crawl toward death.

—for our next sight of his Majesty will show him back from
hunting with a most impatient appetite for dinner! Note, too, the
hint of another Lear, given us in the music of three short words—
the first touch in the play of that peculiar verbal magic Shakespeare could command—when, sated with Goneril's and Regan's
flattery, he turns to his Cordelia with

> Now, our joy . . .

But Lear must leave this first scene as he entered it, more a magnificent portent than a man.

He has doffed his kingship; free from its trappings, how the
native genius of the man begins to show! It flashes on us as might
the last outbursts of some near-extinct volcano. He is old and
uncertain; but a mighty man, never a mere tyrant divested of
power. He has genius, warped and random genius though it may
be, and to madness, as will appear, very near allied. And Shakespeare's art lies in showing us this in nothing he does—for what
he does now is foolish—but in every trivial thing that he is. All
the action of the scene of the return from hunting, all his sur-
roundings are staged to this end. The swift exchanges with the
disguised Kent and their culmination:

> Dost thou know me, fellow?
> No, sir, but you have that in your countenance which I would
> fain call master.
> What's that?
> Authority.

—his encounter with the pernickity jack-in-office Oswald, and
with the frail, whimsical Fool who mockingly echoes his own

passionate whimsies; all this helps set in motion and sets off a new and livelier, a heartier Lear. Not that Shakespeare bates us one jot of the old man's stiff-necked perversities. He no more asks our sympathy on easy terms for him than will Lear yield an inch to Goneril's reasonable requests. A hundred useless knights about the house—even though, from their master's point of view, they were men of choice and rarest parts—must have been a burden. Lear's striking Oswald really was an outrage; after due complaint Goneril would doubtless have reproved his impertinence—for all that she had prompted it! Even with the petted Fool, and in the very midst of the petting, out there snaps

Take heed, sirrah, the whip!

We need look for no tractable virtues in him.

The play's adopted story has its appointed way to go, but here begins the way of Lear's soul's agony and salvation as Shakespeare is to blaze it. The change in him shows first in the dialogue with the attendant knight and the delicate strokes which inform it. The knight, dispatched to bid that mongrel Oswald come back, returns only to report the fellow's round answer that he would not. "He would not!" flashes Lear at the unbelievable phrase. But when, picking his words—as, if you were not a Kent (and there had been room at best for but one Kent at Court), no doubt you learned to do with Lear—the knight hints hesitatingly at trouble, the quiet response comes:

> Thou but remember'st me of mine own conception: I have per-ceived a most faint neglect of late; which I have rather blamed as mine own jealous curiosity, than as a very pretence and purpose of unkindness: I will look further into't. But where's my fool? I have not seen him this two days.
>
> Since my young lady's going into France, sir, the fool hath much pined away.
>
> No more of that; I have noted it well. Go you, and tell my daughter I would speak with her. Go you, call hither my fool. O! you sir, you sir, come you hither, sir!

—this last to the mongrel Oswald who has appeared again. But Lear—can this be the Lear of the play's first scene?—to be turning his knight's "great abatement of kindness" to "a most faint neg-lect," and blaming, even so, his own jealous curiosity for noting it! But the Fool's grief for Cordelia he has noted well. Lest it echo too loudly in his proud unhappy heart, with a quick turn he brings the old Lear to his rescue, rasps an order here, an order there, and—takes it out of Oswald.

From now on the picturing of him is lifelike, in that it has all the varied, unexpected, indirect and latent eloquence of life. Shakespeare is at his deftest, his medium at its freest and most supple. Let the interpreter be alert too. This Lear is as quick on the uptake as it is his Fool's business to be. An unnatural quickness in an old man, is it, and some sign of a toppling brain? His silences are as pregnant. He listens and finds cheer in the Fool's chatter and song, throws him an answer or so to keep it alive, snarls now and then like an old lion if a sting goes too deep. Yet his thoughts, we can tell, are away. We must visualize this scene fully and accurately; the Fool caroling, his poor heart being heavy with Cordelia's loss he carols the more; the old king brooding; and Kent ever watchful, with a dog's eyes. Mark the effect of Goneril's appearance before her father, in purposed, sullen muteness; the Fool's speech points it for us, should we be unobservant; then her break into the prepared formality of verse, as this verse will seem, capping the loose prose of the scene and the Fool's rhyming. Mark, too, the cold kingliness of Lear's four words, all his response to her careful address:

> Are you our daughter?

He resorts to irony, the fine mind's weapon, which blunts itself upon the stupid—for Goneril is stupid, and she has stupidity's stubborn strength. But when the storm of Lear's wrath does break, I think she inwardly shakes a little.

> You strike my people, and your disordered rabble
> Make servants of their betters.

sounds like scared bravado. She can wait, though, for the storm to pass; and, for the moment, it does pass in senile self-reproaches. A few more such futile outbursts, she is confident, and the extravagant old tyrant will be spent and tame enough. But, suddenly, the servants are dismissed and she is alone with husband and father. And her father, rigid, transformed, and with slow, calm, dreadful strength, is calling down the gods' worst curse upon her.

> Hear, Nature, hear! dear goddess, hear!
> Suspend thy purpose if thou didst intend
> To make this creature fruitful! . . .

The actor who will rail and rant this famous passage may know his own barnstorming business, but he is no interpreter of Shakespeare. The merely superficial effect of its deadlier quiet, lodged between two whirlwinds of Lear's fury, should be obvious. But its dramatic purpose far outpasses that. Not indifferently did Shakespeare make this a pagan play, and deprive its argument of comfortable faith in virtue rewarded, here or hereafter. And it is upon this deliberate invocation of ill that we pass into spiritual darkness. The terror of it moves Albany rather than Goneril, whom, indeed, nothing is ever to move. But as he rouses himself to plead against it Lear is gone.[11]

Now havoc begins in him. We have his raging, distracted return, tears of helpless despair punctuating hysterical threats; later the stamping, muttering impatience of his wait for his horses. We know that he sets out on a long hard ride, dinnerless after his hunting. Later we learn that the journey was wasted; he had to post on to Gloucester's. Did he ride through the night without rest or pause? Shakespeare is hunting both Lear and the play's action hard and using every device to do it.

Yet the next day when he reaches Gloucester's house—this old man past eighty, and physically we should suppose near exhaustion —he is master of himself, is his most regal self again.[12] We are given the scene with Kent awaked in the stocks to show it.

> Ha!
> Makest thou this shame thy pastime?

All the old dignity in this; there follows the brusque familiar give-and-take which true authority never fears to practice with its dependents; then again the majestic

---

[11] The "Away, away," is thus spoken to the propitiatory Albany, and has no reference to the servants, who have already been sent off, nor, I think, to Lear's own departure. The point is disputable, no doubt, and I would not go to the stake for my reading of it. The Quartos have "Go, go, my people" repeated, as if his first order had not been obeyed. I must leave it to better judges of their origin and value to say whether this is mere muddlement of text. But, even if it is not, the Folio's change of phrase might cover a change of meaning too.

[12] But the outward signs of exhaustion must begin to be upon him.

Resolve me, with all modest haste, which way
Thou might'st deserve, or they impose, this usage
Coming from us.

and the iron self-control in which the shameful tale is heard.
When the tale is ended he still stands silent, while the Fool pipes
for us an artless mockery (the art of this!) of his bitter and ominous thoughts. Regan too, Regan too! The grief of disillusion has
now become physical pain to him,

O, how this mother swells up toward my heart;
Hysterica passio! down, thou climbing sorrow!

But he masters it.

Where is this daughter? . . .
Follow me not; stay here.

And, solitary in his pride, he goes to face and prove the worst.

If the play, with the invocation of the curse upon Goneril, entered an arena of anarchy and darkness, Lear himself is to pass
now from personal grievance to the taking upon him, as great
natures may, the imagined burden of the whole world's sorrow—
and if his nature breaks under it, what wonder! And Shakespeare
brings about this transition from malediction to martyrdom with
great art, by contrivance direct and indirect, by strokes broad and
subtle; nor ever—his art in this at its greatest—does he turn his
Lear from a man into an ethical proposition. The thing is
achieved—as the whole play is achieved—in terms of humanity,
and according to the rubric of drama.

Lear comes back with Gloucester; the well-meaning Gloucester,
whose timid tact is the one thing least likely to placate him. He is
struggling with himself, with the old tyrannic temper, with his
newfound knowledge of himself, with his body's growing weakness. He is like a great oak tree, torn at the roots, blown this way
and that. When the half-veiled insolence of Regan's and Cornwall's greeting must, one would think, affront him, a pathetic
craving for affection peeps through. When he once more finds
refuge in irony, it is to turn the edge of it against himself. But
with four quick shocks—his sudden recall of the outrage upon his
servant, the sound of a trumpet, the sight of Oswald, the sight of
Goneril—he is brought to a stand and to face the realities arrayed
against him. This must be made very plain to us. On the one side

stand Goneril and Regan and Cornwall in all authority. The
perplexed Gloucester hovers a little apart. On the other side
is Lear, the Fool at his feet, and his one servant, disarmed,
freed but a minute since behind him. Things are at their
issue. His worst errors, after all, have partaken of nobility; he has
scorned policy. He has given himself, helpless, into these carnal
hands. He will abide, then, as nobly the fate he has courted. Note
the single touch of utter scorn for the cur Cornwall, who, the
moment looking likely, takes credit for those stocks.

> I set him there, sir; but his own disorders
> Deserved much less advancement.
>   You! Did you!

But all consequences he'll abide, even welcome, he'll abjure his
curses, run from one ingrate daughter to the other, implore and
bargain, till the depth is sounded and he stands at last surrendered,
and level in his helplessness and deprivation with the least of his
fellow-men.

> GONERIL.   Hear me, my lord,
>   What need you five-and-twenty, ten, or five,
>   To follow in a house where twice so many
>   Have a command to tend you?
> REGAN.   What need one?
> LEAR. O! reason not the need; our basest beggars
>   Are in the poorest thing superfluous:
>   Allow not nature more than nature needs,
>   Man's life is cheap as beast's. . . .
>   But, for true need—
>   You heavens, give me that patience, patience I need!
>   You see me here, you gods, a poor old man
>   As full of grief as age, wretched in both!

"O! reason not the need . . ."! This abandoning of the struggle
and embracing of misfortune is a turning point of the play, a
salient moment in the development of Lear's character, and its
significance must be marked. He is now at the nadir of his fortunes; the tragic heights are at hand.

It may be thought that by emphasizing so many minor points
of stagecraft the great outlines of play and character will be
obscured. But while Shakespeare projects greatly, asking from his
interpreters a simplicity of response, lending them greatness by

virtue of this convention that passes the play's material through the sole crucible of their speech and action, he yet saves them alive, so to speak—not stultified in an attempt to overpass their own powers nor turned to mere mouthpieces of mighty lines—by constant references to the commonplace (we noted more of them in discussing the methods of the dialogue). He invigorates his play's action by keeping its realities upon a battleground where any and every sort of stroke may tell.

Thus there now follows the tense passage in which Goneril, Regan and Cornwall snuff the impending storm and find good reason for ill-doing. What moralists! Regan with her

> O! sir, to wilful men,
> The injuries that they themselves procure
> Must be their schoolmasters.

Cornwall, with his

> Shut up your doors, my lord; 'tis a wild night:
> My Regan counsels well; come out of the storm.

This is surely the very voice—though the tones may be harsh—of respectability and common sense? And what a prelude to the "high engender'd battles" now imminent! Before battle is joined, however, the note of Kent is interposed to keep the play's story going its more pedestrian way and to steady us against the imaginative turmoil pending. This use of Kent is masterly; and, in the storm-scenes themselves, the contrasting use of the Fool, feeble, fantastic, pathetic, a foil to Lear, a foil to the storm—what more incongruous sight conceivable than such a piece of Court tinsel so drenched and buffeted!—is more than masterly.

But it is upon Lear's own progress that all now centers, upon his passing from that royal defiance of the storm to the welcomed shelter of the hovel. He passes by the road of patience:

> No, I will be the pattern of all patience;
> I will say nothing.

of—be it noted—a thankfulness that he is at last simply

> a man
> More sinn'd against than sinning . . .

to the humility of

> My wits begin to turn.
> Come on, my boy. How dost, my boy? Art cold?
> I am cold myself. Where is this straw, my fellow?
> The art of our necessities is strange
> That can make vile things precious. Come, your hovel. . . .

and, a little later yet, mind and body still further strained towards breaking point, to the gentle dignity, when Kent would make way for him—to the more than kingly dignity of

> Prithee, go in thyself: seek thine own ease.
> This tempest will not give me leave to ponder
> On things would hurt me more. But I'll go in:
> In, boy; go first.[18]

Now comes the crowning touch of all:

> I'll pray, and then I'll sleep.

In the night's bleak exposure he kneels down, like a child at bedtime, to pray.

> Poor naked wretches, wheresoe'er you are,
> That bide the pelting of this pitiless storm,
> How shall your houseless heads and unfed sides,
> Your loop'd and window'd raggedness, defend you
> From seasons such as these? O, I have ta'en
> Too little care of this! Take physic, pomp;
> Expose thyself to feel what wretches feel,
> That thou mayst shake the superflux to them,
> And show the heavens more just.

To this haven of the spirit has he come, the Lear of unbridled power and pride. And how many dramatists, could they have achieved so much, would have been content to leave him here! Those who like their drama rounded and trim might approve of such a finish, which would leave us a play more compassable in performance no doubt. But the wind of a harsher doctrine is

---

[18] There are practical reasons for postponing the entering of the hovel by a scene. For Kent to lead Lear elsewhere fits both with the agitated movement of the action and the freedom of Elizabethan stage method. It enables Shakespeare both to relieve the high tension of the storm-scenes and to provide for the continuity of the Gloucester-Edmund story. And he takes advantage of all this to show us some further battering at Lear's sanity. Note in particular the ominously broken thoughts and sentences of the end of the speech to Kent just before the hovel is reached; and these, as ominously, are set between connected, reasoned passages.

blowing through Shakespeare. Criticism, as we have seen, is apt to fix upon the episode of the storm as the height of his attempt and the point of his dramatic defeat; but it is this storm of the mind here beginning upon which he expends skill and imagination most recklessly till inspiration has had its will of him; and the drama of desperate vision ensuing it is hard indeed for actors to reduce to the positive medium of their art—without reducing it to ridicule. The three coming scenes of Lear's madness show us Shakespeare's art at its boldest. They pass beyond the needs of the plot, they belong to a larger synthesis.[14] Yet the means they employ are simple enough; of a kind of absolute simplicity, indeed.

The boldest and simplest is the provision of Poor Tom, that living instance of all rejection. Here, under our eyes, is Lear's new vision of himself.

> What! have his daughters brought him to this pass?
> Could'st thou save nothing? Did'st thou give them all?

Side by side stand the noble old man, and the naked, scarce human wretch.

> Is man no more than this? Consider him well. Thou owest the worm no silk, the beast no hide, the sheep no wool, the cat no perfume. Ha! here's three on's are sophisticated; thou art the thing itself; unaccommodated man is no more but such a poor, bare, forked animal as thou art. Off, off, you lendings! Come; unbutton here.

Here is a volume of argument epitomized as only drama can epitomize it, flashed on us by word and action combined. And into this, one might add, has Shakespeare metamorphosed the didactics of those old Moralities which were the infancy of his art.

> What! hath your grace no better company?

gasps poor Gloucester, bewailing at once the King's wrongs and his own, as he offers shelter from the storm. But Lear, calmness itself now, will only pace up and down, arm in arm with this refuse of humanity:

---

[14] It is worth noting that the Folio cuts out the lunatic trial of Regan and Goneril. This episode proves so admirable on the stage that it is hard to suppose Shakespeare's actor failed to make it effective. But if it was a question of time and a choice between two scenes, doubtless his audience would be supposed to prefer the rhetoric of the storm.

Noble philosopher, your company.

—nor will he seek shelter without him. So they reach the outhouse, all of his own castle that Gloucester dare offer. What a
group! Kent, sturdy and thrifty of words; Gloucester, tremulous;
the bedraggled and exhausted Fool; and Lear, magnificently
courteous and deliberate, keeping close company with his gibber-
ing fellow-man.[15]

They are in shelter. Lear is silent; till the Fool—himself never
overfitted, we may suppose, in body or mind for the rough and
tumble of the world—rallies, as if to celebrate their safety, to a
semblance of his old task. Edgar, for his own safety's sake, must
play Poor Tom to the life now. Kent has his eyes on his master,
watching him—at what new fantastic trick? The old king is setting two joint-stools side by side; they are Regan and Goneril,
and the Fool and the beggar are to pass judgment upon them.

The lunatic mummery of the trial comes near to something we
might call pure drama—as one speaks of pure mathematics or
pure music—since it cannot be rendered into other terms than its
own. Its effect depends upon the combination of the sound and
meaning of the words and the sight of it being brought to bear
as a whole directly upon our sensibility. The sound of the dialogue
matters almost more than its meaning. Poor Tom and the Fool
chant antiphonally; Kent's deep and kindly tones tell against the
higher, agonized, weakening voice of Lear. But the chief significance is in the show. Where Lear, such a short while since, sat in
his majesty, there sit the Fool and the outcast, with Kent whom
he banished beside them; and he, witless, musters his failing
strength to beg justice upon a joint-stool. Was better justice done,
the picture ironically asks, when he presided in majesty and
sanity and power?

But what, as far as Lear is concerned, is to follow? You cannot
continue the development of a character in terms of lunacy—in
darkness, illuminated by whatever brilliant flashes of lightning.
Nor can a madman well dominate a play's action. From this
moment Lear no longer is a motive force; and the needs of the
story—the absolute needs of the character—would be fulfilled if,
from this exhausted sleep upon the poor bed in the outhouse, he

---

[15] And Kent is unknown to Lear and Edgar to his father, as we shall sufficiently
remember.

only woke to find Cordelia at his side. But Shakespeare contrives
another scene of madness for him, and one which lifts the play's
argument to a yet rarer height. It is delayed; and the sense of
redundancy is avoided partly by keeping Lear from the stage
altogether for a while, a short scene interposed sufficiently remind-
ing us of him.[16]

His reappearance is preluded—with what consonance!—by the
fantastically imaginative episode of Gloucester's fall from the cliff.
There also is Edgar, the aura of Poor Tom about him still. Suddenly Lear breaks in upon them.[17] The larger dramatic value of
the ensuing scene can hardly be overrated. For in it, in this
encounter between mad Lear and blind Gloucester, the sensual
man robbed of his eyes, and the despot, the light of his mind put
out, Shakespeare's sublimation of the two old stories is consum-
mated. No moral is preached to us. It is presented as it was when
king and beggar fraternized in the storm and beggar and Fool
were set on the bench of justice, and we are primarily to *feel* the
significance. Yet this does not lack interpretation; less explicit than
when Lear, still sane, could read the lesson of the storm, clearer
than was the commentary on the mock trial. It is Edgar here that
sets us an example of sympathetic listening. His asides enforce it,
and the last one:

> O! matter and impertinency mixed,
> Reason in madness!

will reproach us if we have not understood. The train of fancies
fired by the first sight of Gloucester, with its tragically comic

---

[16] In the Quarto another preceding scene is also concerned with him.

[17] *Mad*, says the stage direction, and no more; the usual *fantastically dressed
with wild flowers* is Capel's addition. But something of the sort is justified by
Cordelia's speech in the earlier scene. And the dramatic purpose of them is plain:
to emphasize the contrast between this and our last sight of him amid the barren
wildness of the heath and the storm.

There are signs, it may be noted, that this Gloucester-Lear encounter is a
second thought on Shakespeare's part. Apart from its redundance to the action, the
Gloucester-Edgar scene is complete without it; and originally, one would guess,
Gloucester's

> Henceforth I'll bear
> Affliction till it do cry out itself
> 'Enough, enough!' and die.

was followed directly by Edgar's

> Well pray you, father!

Ha! Goneril with a white beard!

(Goneril, disguised, pursuing him still!) asks little gloss.

> They flattered me like a dog. . . . To say 'Ay' and 'No' to every-
> thing I said! . . . When the rain came to wet me once and the
> wind to make me chatter, when the thunder would not peace at
> my bidding, there I found 'em, there I smelt 'em out. Go to, they
> are not men o' their words; they told me I was everything; 'tis a
> lie, I am not ague-proof.

Gloucester's dutiful

> Is't not the king?

begins to transform him in those mad eyes. And madness sees a
Gloucester there that sanity had known and ignored.

> I pardon that man's life: What was thy cause?
> Adultery?
> Thou shalt not die: die for adultery! No:
> The wren goes to't, and the small gilded fly
> Does lecher in my sight.
> Let copulation thrive; for Gloucester's bastard son
> Was kinder to his father than my daughters
> Got 'tween the lawful sheets.

Gloucester knows better; but how protest so to the mere erratic
voice? Besides which there is only the kindly stranger-peasant
near. A slight unconscious turn of the sightless eyes toward him, a
simple gesture—unseen—in response from Edgar, patiently biding
his time, will illuminate the irony and the pathos.

Does the mad mind pass logically from this to some uncanny
prevision of the ripening of new evil in Regan and Goneril? Had
it in its sanity secretly surmised what lay beneath the moral surface of their lives, so ready to emerge?

> Behold yon simpering dame
> Whose face between her forks presageth snow;
> That minces virtue and does shake the head
> To hear of pleasure's name;
> The fitchew, nor the soiled horse, goes to't
> With a more riotous appetite.[18]

---

[18] The (superficial) inappositeness of this passage is quoted nowadays as evidence of Shakespeare's morbid occupation, about now, with the uncleaner aspects
of sex. But it is by no means inapposite to the larger moral scheme of the play.
Goneril's lust has become an important factor in the action. Shakespeare cannot

But a man—so lunatic logic runs—must free himself from the tyrannies of the flesh if he is to see the world clearly:

> Give me an ounce of civet, good apothecary, to sweeten my imagination.

And then a blind man may see the truth of it, so he tells the ruined Gloucester:

> Look with thine ears: see how yond justice rails upon yond simple thief. Hark in thine ear: change places, and, handy-dandy, which is the justice, which is the thief? Thou hast seen a farmer's dog bark at a beggar? . . . And the creature run from the cur? There thou might'st behold the great image of authority; a dog's obeyed in office.

It is the picture of the mock trial given words. But with a difference! There is no cry now for vengeance on the wicked. For what are we that we should smite them?

> Thou rascal beadle, hold thy bloody hand!
> Why dost thou lash that whore? Strip thine own back;
> That hotly lust'st to use her in that kind
> For which thou whip'st her. The usurer hangs the cozener.
> Through tattered clothes small vices do appear;
> Robes and furr'd gowns hide all. Plate sin with gold,
> And the strong lance of justice hurtless breaks;
> Arm it in rags, a pigmy's straw doth pierce it.

Shakespeare has led Lear to compassion for sin as well as suffering, has led him mad to where he could not hope to lead him sane —to where sound common sense will hardly let us follow him:

> None does offend, none, I say, none.

To a deep compassion for mankind itself.

> I know thee well enough; thy name is Gloucester;
> Thou must be patient; we came crying hither:
> Thou know'st the first time that we smell the air
> We wawl and cry. I will preach to thee: mark. . . .
> When we are born, we cry that we are come
> To this great stage of fools.

---

give much space to its developments, nor does he care to set the boys acting women to deal directly and elaborately with such matters. So he uses, I think, this queer intuition of the mad mind as a mirror in which the vileness is reflected and dilated.

This afterpart of Lear's madness may be redundant, then, to the strict action of the play, but to its larger issues it is most germane. It is perhaps no part of the play that Shakespeare set out to write. The play that he found himself writing would be how much the poorer without it!

The simple perfection of the scene that restores Lear to Cordelia one can leave unsullied by comment. What need of any? Let the producer only note that there is reason in the Folio's stage direction:

> *Enter Lear in a chair carried by servants.*

For when he comes to himself it is to find that he is royally attired and as if seated on his throne again. It is from this throne that he totters to kneel at Cordelia's feet.[19] Note, too, the pain of his response to Kent's

> In your own kingdom, sir.
>
> Do not abuse me.

Finally, Lear must pass from the scene with all the ceremony due to royalty: not mothered—please!—by Cordelia.

Cordelia found again and again lost, what is left for Lear but to die? But for her loss, however, his own death might seem to us an arbitrary stroke; since the old Lear, we may say, is already dead. Shakespeare, moreover, has transported him beyond all worldly issues. This is, perhaps, why the action of the battle which will seemingly defeat his fortunes is minimized. What does defeat matter to him—or even victory? It is certainly the key to the meaning of the scene which follows. Cordelia, who would "out-frown false fortune's frown," is ready to face her sisters and to shame them—were there a chance of it!—with the sight of her father's wrongs. But Lear himself has no interest in anything of the sort.

> No, no, no, no! Come, let's away to prison.
> We two alone will sing like birds i' the cage:
> When thou dost ask me blessing, I'll kneel down,
> And ask of thee forgiveness[20]: so we'll live,
> And pray, and sing, and tell old tales, and laugh
> At gilded butterflies, and hear poor rogues
> Talk of court news. . . .

---

[19] Shakespeare kept—and transformed—this piece of business from the old play; for Cordelia kneels, too, of course. It should be given its full value.

[20] That scene in the old play haunted Shakespeare.

He has passed beyond care for revenge or success, beyond even the questioning of rights and wrongs. Better indeed to be oppressed, if so you can be safe from contention. Prison will bring him freedom.

> Upon such sacrifices, my Cordelia,
> The gods themselves throw incense. Have I caught thee?
> He that parts us shall bring a brand from heaven
> And fire us hence like foxes. Wipe thine eyes;
> The good years shall devour them, flesh and fell,
> Ere they shall make us weep: we'll see 'em starve first.

Lear's death, upon one ground or another, is artistically inevitable. Try to imagine his survival; no further argument will be needed. The death of Cordelia has been condemned as a wanton outrage upon our feelings and so as an aesthetic blot upon the play. But the dramatic mind that was working to the tune of

> As flies to wanton boys are we to the gods;
> They kill us for their sport.

was not likely to be swayed by sentiment. The tragic truth about life, to the Shakespeare that wrote *King Lear*, included its capricious cruelty. And what meeter sacrifice to this than Cordelia? Besides, as we have seen, he must provide this new Lear with a tragic determinant, since "the great rage . . . is kill'd in him," which precipitated catastrophe for the old Lear. And what but Cordelia's loss would suffice?

We have already set Lear's last scene in comparison with his first; it will be worth while to note a little more particularly the likeness and the difference. The same commanding figure; he bears the body of Cordelia as lightly as ever he carried robe, crown and scepter before. All he has undergone has not so bated his colossal strength but that he could kill her murderer with his bare hands.

> I kill'd the slave that was a-hanging thee.
> Tis true, my lords, he did.

says the officer in answer to their amazed looks. Albany, Edgar. Kent and the rest stand silent and intent around him; Regan and Goneril are there, silent too. He stands, with the limp body close clasped, glaring blankly at them for a moment. When speech is torn from him, in place of the old kingly rhetoric we have only the horrible, half human

Howl, howl, howl, howl!

Who these are, for all their dignity and martial splendor, for all the respect they show him, he neither knows nor cares. They are men of stone and murderous traitors; though, after a little, through the mist of his suffering, comes a word for Kent. All his world, of power and passion and will, and the wider world of thought over which his mind in its ecstasy had ranged, is narrowed now to Cordelia; and she is dead in his arms.

Here is the clue to the scene; this terrible concentration upon the dead, and upon the unconquerable fact of death. This thing was Cordelia; she was alive, she is dead. Here is human tragedy brought to its simplest terms, fit ending to a tragic play that has seemed to outleap human experience. From power of intellect and will, from the imaginative sweep of madness, Shakespeare brings Lear to this; to no moralizing nor high thoughts, but just to

> She's gone for ever.
> I know when one is dead and when one lives;
> She's dead as earth. Lend me a looking-glass;
> If that her breath will mist or stain the stone,
> Why, then she lives.

Lacking a glass, he catches at a floating feather. That stirs on her lips; a last mockery. Kent kneels by him to share his grief. Then to the bystanders comes the news of Edmund's death; the business of life goes forward, as it will, and draws attention from him for a moment. But what does he heed? When they turn back to him he has her broken body in his arms again.

> And my poor fool is hang'd. No, no, no life!
> Why should a dog, a horse, a rat, have life,
> And thou no breath at all? Thou'lt come no more,
> Never, never, never, never, never!
> Pray you, undo this button; thank you, sir.
> Do you see this? Look on her, look, her lips,
> Look there, look there![21]

---

[21] Bradley has an admirable note upon this passage, just such a fine piece of perception as we expect from him. Lear, he says, at the very last, thinks that Cordelia lives, and dies of the joy of it.

GONERIL, REGAN AND CORDELIA

Shakespeare's point of departure for all three is that of the crude old story. Moreover, with regard to Goneril and Regan he is quite content to assume—we shrink from the assumption nowadays—that there are really wicked people in the world. That admitted, these two exemplars of the fact are lifelike enough. Their aspect may be determined by the story's needs, but their significance does not end here; and, within the limits afforded them, they develop freely and naturally, each in her own way.

Likeness and difference are marked from the beginning. They are both realists. Their father wants smooth speech of them and they give it, echoing his very phrases and tones. They ignore Cordelia's reproaches; she is exiled and in disgrace, so they safely may. Left alone together (and the drop here from verse to prose seems to bring us with something of a bump to the plain truth about them), they are under no illusions at all, we find, about their own good fortune.

> he always loved our sister most; and with what poor judg-
> ment he hath now cast her off appears too grossly.

There are few things more unlovely than the passionless appraise-ment of evil and our profit in it. They are as wide-awake to the chances of trouble ahead; but while Regan would wait and see, Goneril means to go to meet it.

If the quarrel between King Lear and his two daughters had been brought into the law courts, counsels' speeches for Regan and Goneril would have been interesting. But what a good case Goneril makes for herself unaided! The setting-on of Oswald to provoke Lear might, one supposes, have been kept out of the evidence. True, the reservation of a hundred knights was a defi-nite condition of his abdication. But their behavior was impeach-able; it may well have been if Lear's own treatment of Oswald set them an example. He was almost in his dotage; unbalanced certainly. His outbursts of ironic rage, the cursing of Goneril, his subsequent ravings—his whole conduct shows him unfit to look after himself. For his own sake, then, how much better for his daughters' servants to wait on him! And Regan, though she needs Goneril's prompting, makes an even better case of it; the weaker nature is the more plausible. A jury of men and women of com-

mon sense might well give their verdict against Lear; and we can
hear the judge ruling upon the one point of law in his favor with
grave misgiving that he is doing him no good. How then can we
call Regan and Goneril double-dyed fiends? They played the
hypocrite for a kingdom; but which of us might not? Having
got what they wanted and more than they expected they found
good excuse for not paying the price for it. Like failings have been
known in the most reputable people. Their conduct so far, it could
be argued, has been eminently respectable, level-headed and
worldly-wise. They do seem somewhat hard-hearted, but that is
all. Says the broken, mad old king:

> let them anatomize Regan, see what breeds about her heart.
> Is there any cause in nature that makes these hard hearts?

But from now on the truth about them grows patent. Does
prosperity turn their heads? It releases hidden devils. When Gloucester's defection is discovered they waste no words.

> Hang him instantly.
> Pluck out his eyes.

And the weaker Regan grows the more violent of the two; she
turns crueler even than that bloody wolf, Cornwall, her husband.
For amid the scuffling a little later she can think to tell Gloucester
that his own son has betrayed him; and even as he faces her,
blinded and bleeding, she can jeer at him.

The devil of lust comes now to match with the devil of cruelty.
Goneril has hardly seen Edmund but she marks him down with
those

> strange œilliads and most speaking looks . . .

—which rouse Regan to jealousy as quickly. In their plot upon
their father they were clever enough, self-controlled, subtle. But,
the beast let loose in them, they turn reckless, shameless, foolish.
Regan, with a little law on her side, presumes on it; so Goneril
poisons her as she might a rat. And the last note of Goneril is one
of devilish pride.

> Say, if I do, the laws are mine, not thine:
> Who can arraign me for it?

Flinging this at her husband when he confronts her with the proof
that she meant to have his life, she departs to take her own.

We may see, then, in Goneril and Regan, evil triumphant, self-degrading and self-destructive. It may also be that, from beginning to end, Shakespeare, for his part, sees little to choose between hot lust and murdering hand and the hard heart, in which all is rooted.

It will be a fatal error to present Cordelia as a meek saint. She has more than a touch of her father in her. She is as proud as he is, and as obstinate, for all her sweetness and her youth. And, being young, she answers uncalculatingly with pride to his pride even as later she answers with pity to his misery. To miss this likeness between the two is to miss Shakespeare's first important dramatic effect; the mighty old man and the frail child, confronted, and each unyielding.

> So young and so untender?
> So young, my lord, and true.

And they both have the right of it, after all. If age owes some tolerance to youth, it may be thought too that youth owes to age and fatherhood something more—and less—than the truth. But she has courage, has Cordelia, amazing courage. Princess though she be, it is no small matter to stand her ground before Lear, throned in the plenitude of his power, to stand up to him without effort, explanation or excuse. Nor does she wince at the penalty, nor to the end utter one pleading word. Nor, be it noted, does Kent, who is of her temper, ask pity for her. His chief concern is to warn Lear against his own folly and its consequences.[22] It is her strength of mind he emphasizes and praises.

> The gods to their dear shelter take thee, maid,
> That justly think'st and hast most rightly said!

Nor would she, apparently, open her mouth again to her father but that she means her character shall be cleared. And even this approach to him is formal and uncompromising:

> I yet beseech your majesty . . .

She does (Shakespeare keeps her human) slip in, as if it hardly mattered, a dozen words of vindication:

---

[22] And certain small alterations from Quarto to Folio emphasize this.

> . . . since what I well intend,
> I'll do't before I speak.

Yet, lest even that should seem weakness, she nullifies its effect for
a finish. Nor does Lear respond, nor exonerate her except by a
noncommittal growl. Still, she is not hard.

> The jewels of our father, with wash'd eyes
> Cordelia leaves you. . . .

Shakespeare has provided in this encounter between Cordelia
and Lear that prime necessity of drama, clash of character; that
sharpest clash, moreover, of like in opposition to like. He has
added wonder and beauty by setting these twin spirits in noble
and contrasted habitations. Pride unchecked in Lear has grown
monstrous and diseased with his years. In her youth it shows
unspoiled, it is in flower. But it is the same pride.

The technical achievement in Shakespeare's staging of Cordelia
is his gain of a maximum effect by a minimum of means. It is a
triumph of what may be called "placing." The character itself
has, to begin with, that vitality which positive virtues give. Cordelia is never in doubt about herself; she has no vagaries, she is
what she is all circumstances apart, what she says seems to come
new-minted from her mind, and our impression of her is as
clean cut. Add to this her calm and steadfast isolation among the
contending or subservient figures of that first scene—and the fact,
of course, that from this very thrift of herself the broadcast violence of the play's whole action springs—then we see how, with
but a reminder of her here and there, Shakespeare could trust to
her reappearance after long delay, no jot of her importance nor of
our interest in her bated. Indeed, if the Folio text gives us in the
main his own reconsiderations, he found his first care to reinstate
her in our sympathy a scene before she reappears to be needless.[23]
But at this point the play itself is beginning to have need of her
return. Somehow its intolerable agonies must be eased; and amid
the dreadful flux our memory of her certainty abides.

There is not, at any time, much to explain in Cordelia. Nor does
she now herself protest her love and expand her forgiveness. She
has not changed; elaboration would only falsify her. Not that she

---

23 Act IV, Scene iii.

is by nature taciturn; she can resolve the harmonies of her mind,
and Shakespeare gives a flowing music to them.

> Was this a face
> To be opposed against the warring winds?
> To stand against the deep dread-bolted thunder?
> In the most terrible and nimble stroke
> Of quick cross lightning? to watch—poor perdu!
> With this thin helm? Mine enemy's dog,
> Though he had bit me, should have stood that night
> Against my fire.

But even this is not spoken to Lear. To him she still says little. It
is as if speech itself were not a simple or genuine enough thing
for the expressing of her deep heart. And her

> No cause, no cause!

when he would welcome her reproaches, is not at all the kindly,
conventional, superior "Let's forget it" of the morally offended. It
is but the complement of that "Nothing" which cost her a kingdom, and as true of her in its tenderness as the other was true. For
the simple secret of Cordelia's nature is that she does not see
things from the standpoint of her own gain or loss. She did not
beg, she does not bargain. She can give as she could lose, keeping
a quiet mind. It is no effort to her to love her father better than
herself. Yet this supremest virtue, as we count it, is no gain to him;
we must note this too. Her wisdom of heart showed her Regan
and Goneril as they were; yet it was an inarticulate wisdom and
provoked evil in Lear, and could but hold her bound in patience
till the evil was purged. Is there, then, an impotence in such good-
ness, lovely as we find it? And is this why Shakespeare lets her
slip out of the play a few scenes later to her death, as if, for all
her beauty of spirit, she were not of so much account? Neither
good fortune nor ill can touch Cordelia herself; this is her strength
and her weakness both.

> For thee, oppressed king, am I cast down;
> Myself could else outfrown false fortune's frown. . . .

she says; and so she could, we are sure. Then she falls into dumbness—into such a dumbness as was her first undoing—and passes,
silent, from our sight.

KENT

Here is another positive, absolute being; he, Lear and Cordelia make a trinity of them. He has not Lear's perilous intellect nor Cordelia's peace of soul. His dominant quality is his unquestioning courage; akin to this the selflessness which makes it as easy for him to be silent as to speak. And he springs from Shakespeare's imagination all complete; full-flavored and consistent from the first. Surer sign yet of his author's certainty about him is the natural inconsistency of the man as we see him. Through the first three acts there is never a stroke in the drawing of Kent which is merely conventional, nor yet an uncertain one. But neither is there one which, however unexpected, need perplex us. And for a small sign of Shakespeare's confidence in the sufficiency of his creature, see the shrewd critical thrust which he lets Cornwall have at him:

> This is some fellow,
> Who, having been praised for bluntness, doth affect
> A saucy roughness. . . .

Even though it be a Cornwall disparaging a Kent, the thrust is shrewd enough for Shakespeare not to risk it unless he is confident that Kent's credit with the audience is firm.

This variety and apparent inconsistency give great vitality. From the Kent of the first scene, quick of eye, frank at a question:

> Is not this your son, my lord?

impatient at half answers:

> I cannot conceive you.

yet tolerant, discreetly courteous, dry, self-contained:

> I cannot wish the fault undone, the issue of it being so proper.

but gentle and kindly too:

> I must love you and sue to know you better.

—from this we pass without warning to the impetuous outburst against Lear; and unmannerly though this may be, it is still dignified, collected and cool. From this to the Kent of the borrowed accents—but never more himself than in his disguise, to the man of

What would'st thou?
Service.
Who would'st thou serve?
You.
Dost thou know me, fellow?
No, sir; but you have that in your countenance which I would
fain call master.
What's that?
Authority.

to the Kent of the tripping of Oswald; and, at their next meeting,
with Oswald so unwary as to ask him

What dost thou know me for?

to the Kent of

> A knave, a rascal, an eater of broken meats; a base, proud,
> shallow, beggarly, three-suited, hundred-pound, filthy, worsted-
> stocking knave; a lily-livered, action-taking knave; a whoreson,
> glass-gazing, super-serviceable, finical rogue; a one-trunk inherit-
> ing slave; one that wouldst be a bawd in way of good service, and
> art nothing but the composition of a knave, beggar, coward,
> pandar, and the son and heir of a mongrel bitch; one whom I
> will beat into clamorous whining if thou deniest the least syllable
> of thy addition.

to the resourceful, humorous disputant of the scene with Cornwall
and Regan, and to the philosopher in the stocks, with his

Fortune, good-night; smile once more; turn thy wheel!

Having so opulently endowed him with life, Shakespeare, we
may say, can now afford to be thriftier of attention to him for a
while; he had better be, we might add, or the balance of the
play's interest will go awry. But it is of a piece with the character
that, when misfortune overwhelms Lear, Kent should sink himself in it, that his colorfulness should fade, his humor wane, and
the rest of the play find him tuned to this one key of vigilant
unquestioning service; till he comes to the final simplicity of

I have a journey, sir, shortly to go.
My master calls me, I must not say no.

Nevertheless Shakespeare does seem in Act IV to lose interest in
him, thus straitened, and he keeps him a place in the action care-

lessly enough. Throughout the storm-scenes, of course, his sober,
single-minded concern for the King does but reinforce his dramatic credit; it is, besides, a necessary check to their delirium. He
could have even less to say here, and his very presence would be
a strength. It is like Kent not to fuss as poor Gloucester fusses,
not to talk when he need not, to think of the morrow and do the
best he can meanwhile. Shakespeare allows him—a just economy
—two flashes of emotion; the first when Lear turns to him with

> Wilt break my heart?
> I'd rather break my own . . . .

he says. And once—

> O pity!

No more than that.

It is after he has taken Lear to Dover that, as a character, he
begins to live upon the credit of his past. Shakespeare seems not
quite sure what more he may want of him; he only does not want
him to complicate with his vigorous personality the crowded later
action of the play. What his purpose may be in sustaining his
disguise—

> Pardon, dear madam;
> Yet to be known shortens my made intent:
> My boon I make it that you know me not
> Till time and I think meet.

—is never very clear. But Shakespeare's own purpose here is clear
enough; not to spoil Lear's reconciliation with Cordelia, by adding
to it a recognition of Kent. The couplet with which Kent ends
the scene:

> My point and period will be throughly wrought,
> Or well or ill, as this day's battle's fought.

has in the event neither much significance nor consequence. It is
a safe remark and sounds well. We might suppose (we may do so,
if we like; but in fact an audience will not stop to consider a commentator's point) that Kent is counting, if Lear is defeated, on
serving him still in disguise, when known he could not. But he
does not appear in the battle or the defeat; and this we might
think (if, again, we stopped to think; but while the play is acting

we shall not) as strange as his neglect which had let Lear escape
to wander

> As mad as the vex'd sea; singing aloud . . .

But the simple explanation probably is that Shakespeare finds he
has no more dramatic use for Kent till he can bring him on, the
play all but done, with

> I am come
> To bid my king and master aye good-night.

So he must just keep him in being meanwhile.

That Kent should survive so effectively to the play's end is at
once a tribute to the vitality of his first projection and to the tact
with which Shakespeare can navigate the shallows of his art. And
the actor who can express himself and impress himself upon us
as well by silence as by speech will find no difficulties in the part.[24]

THE FOOL

The Fool can never, of course, be to us what he was to the
play's first audience. For them, Shakespeare's achievement lay in
the double conversion of a stock stage character and a traditional
Court figure to transcendent dramatic use. There are few greater
pleasures in art than to find the familiar made new; but to us
stage Fool and Court Fool alike are strange to start with. Court
Fool has, to be sure, a likely claim to a place in the play, and can
claim a place too in our historical consciousness. Grant the old
King such a favorite: it is good character scheming to contrast
his royal caprices with such spaniel affection; dramatic craft at its
best to leave Lear in adversity this one fantastic remnant of
royalty. This, and much more of intrinsic value, we cannot lose.
But what, from the transcended stage Fool, did Shakespeare gain
besides?

---

[24] If it be said that there is nothing in the Kent of Act IV which, upon analysis,
belies his character, yet this Preface is concerned also with his presentment, and
that is ineffective and even halting. But what of his sudden outburst in Act IV,
Sc. iii:

> It is the stars;
> The stars above us, govern our conditions . . . .

—is this the authentic Kent? And even if Shakespeare were here starting to develop a new phase of the man, he never goes on.

For a masterly analysis of the whole character we should turn to A. C.
Bradley's lecture on *King Lear*.

Elizabethan acting did not inhabit the removed footlight-defended stage of the theater of today, and all its technique and conventions and the illusion it created differ appropriately in consequence; this is the constant theme of these Prefaces, and must be of any study of the staging of Shakespeare plays. But certain effects, however gained, are common to all drama, certain problems recur. A problem in the writing and acting of tragedy is the alternate creating and relaxing of emotional strain; the tenser the strain, the less long can an audience appreciatively endure it. "Comic relief" has a crude sound; but, to some degree and in some form or other, the thing it suggests is a necessity. Greek tragedy had "choric relief"; emotion in the Greek theater was magnified and rarefied at once, and sharp transitions were neither wanted nor workable. Shakespeare had the constant shift of scene and subject, usual in his theater, to help him; and his most strenuous scenes, we may remark, tend to be short ones.[25] We may suppose him ever mindful of the difficulty of keeping the attention of a motley audience fixed, but still alert; and in the body of a scene, if it needs must be a long one, we shall always find what may be called "points of rest and recovery."

But the problem can be stated in other terms. Tragedy, it may be said, takes us out of ourselves; how else can it be enjoyed? A dash of comedy will, by contrast, restore us to ourselves; yet, for the tragedy's sake, the less conscious of the process we are the better. Here lay for Shakespeare, in this play, the histrionic value of the Fool. He wanted no comic relief in the crude sense; but this familiar stage figure, even though turned to tragic purpose, kept for that audience, if insensibly, its traditional hail-fellow quality. Only the dramatic and human value of the character is preserved us for today to the full. Of the effect of the snatches of song and rhyme, the lyric lightening of the epic strength of these scenes, we keep only the most manifest part. The things themselves are queer to us, and this is just what they should not be. And of the friendly feeling, the sense of being at ease with our-

---

[25] This play apart, they are noticeably so in *Macbeth* and in *Antony and Cleopatra*. In *Hamlet* and in *Othello* it may be said they are not. But in *Hamlet* the action is—and characteristically—not consistently strenuous; and the sustaining of the anguish in *Othello* is typical of the tragedy, helps give us the heroic measure of Othello himself.

selves, which the stage Fool, a-straddle between play and audience, could create for the Elizabethans, we save nothing at all. We have felt something of the sort as children perhaps, when, at the Pantomime, after the removed mysteries of the transformation scene, came the harlequinade and the clown, cuddling us up to him with his "Here we are again." It may seem a far cry from red-hot poker and sausages to *King Lear*. But these indigenous attributes of the Fool are the underlying strength of the part once its acting is in question; and it is Shakespeare's use and restraint and disguise of them at once that is so masterly. Out went the character, as we know, from the eighteenth century versions of the play; nor actors nor audience, it was thought, could countenance such an aberration. Macready restored it with many misgivings and gave it to a girl to act. The producer today faces another difficulty. He finds a Fool all etherealized by the higher criticism. His first care, in the part's embodying, must be to see restored as much as may be of its lost aboriginal strength. Its actor must sing like a lark, juggle his words so that the mere skill delights us, and tumble around with all the grace in the world. Satisfy these simpler demands, and the subtleties will have their effect; neglect them, and you might as well try to play tunes on a punctured organ stop.

About the Fool's character in the personal sense there is really not much to be said, though it is a subject upon which the romantic commentator has rejoiced to embroider his own fancies. He is, not a half-wit, but—the old word fits—a "natural"; he does not, that is to say, draw all our practical distinction between sense and nonsense, the wise thing to do, and the unwise. But he lives in a logical world of his own. Lear has petted him as one pets a dog; he shows a dog's fidelity. It is foolish of him, no doubt, to follow his master into such a storm—but, then, he *is* a fool. Shakespeare, having had his dramatic use of him, drops him incontinently; this alone should label the part of merely incidental importance to the scheme of the play. But even this he makes a measure of the human pathos of the creature. We are told by the attendant knight before ever we see him:

> Since my young lady's going into France, sir, the fool
> hath much pined away.
> No more of that; I have noted it well . . . .

Lear answers (lest we should not note it well enough). But not a word more; above all never a hint from this professional jester himself that he has, or has a right to, any feelings of his own. His jests have grown bitterer lately perhaps, to suit with Lear's changing fortunes; yet, for compensation, he is more full of song than ever. And come weal, come woe, he sticks to his job, sticks to it and to his master till the storm batters him into silence. With a ha'porth of warmth and comfort in him, he flickers bravely into jest again. But his task is done now, and he himself pretty well done for. He tells us so in a very short and bitter jest indeed:

> And I'll go to bed at noon.

And this is the last we hear or see of him; and what happens to him thereafter, who knows or cares? Which is quite according to the jesters'—and players'—code of professional honor, and to the common reward of its observance, as Shakespeare, of all men, would know well. To pursue the Fool beyond the play's bounds, to steep him in extraneous sentiment, is to miss the most characteristically dramatic thing about him.

One minor point about the part is yet an important one. The soliloquy with which Act III, Scene ii, is made to end is certainly spurious.[26] Its own incongruity can be left out of the question; its offense against the dramatic situation disallows it. The very heart of this is Lear's new-found care for the shivering drenched creature at his side.

> Come on, my boy. How dost, my boy? Art cold? . . .
> Poor fool and knave, I have one part in my heart
> That's sorry yet for thee.

Shakespeare is incapable—so would any other dramatist in his senses be—of stultifying himself by dispatching Lear from the scene immediately after, and letting him leave the Fool behind him.

GLOUCESTER, EDGAR AND EDMUND

Gloucester and his sons are opposite numbers, as the phrase now goes, to Lear and his daughters. Gloucester himself is the

---

[26] And surely it is time that all editions of Shakespeare put certain passages, whose fraud can be agreed upon, in expurgatorial brackets. We are ready for another—and another sort of—Bowdler.

play's nearest approach to the average sensual man. The civilized
world is full of Gloucesters. In half a dozen short speeches
Shakespeare sets him fully before us: turning elderly but probably still handsome; nice of speech if a little pompous, the accomplished courtier (he seems to be Lear's master of ceremonies);
vain, as his mock modesty shows, but the joking shamelessness
that succeeds it is mainly swagger; an egotist, and blind, knowing
least of what he should know most, of his own two sons.

> He hath been out nine years, and away he shall again.

That carelessly jovial sentence of banishment for Edmund proves
his own death-sentence. Still, who could suspect the modest young
newcomer, making his bow with

> Sir, I shall study deserving.

of having such unpleasant thoughts in mind?

Gloucester, like so many sensual men, is good nature itself, as
long as things go their easy, natural way; but when they fail to he
is upset, rattled. Kent's banishment, the quarrel with Cordelia
and France, and the King's utter recklessness set his mind off at
one tangent and another and make him an easier victim to very
simple deceit. We must not, however, appraise either his simplicity or Edgar's, at this moment, with detachment—for by that
light, no human being, it would seem, between infancy and
dotage, could be so gullible. Shakespeare asks us to allow him
the fact of the deception, even as we have allowed him Lear's
partition of the kingdom. It is his starting point, the dramatist's
"let's pretend," which is as essential to the beginning of a play
as a "let it be granted" to a proposition of Euclid. And, within
bounds, the degree of pretense makes surprisingly little difference. It is what the assumption will commit him to that counts;
once a play's action is under way it must develop as logically as
Euclid, and far more logically than life. The art of the thing is
to reward the spectator for his concession by never presuming on
it; one should rather dress up the unlikely in the likelier. Thus
Shakespeare makes Gloucester, with his pother about "these late
eclipses of the sun and moon," the sort of man who might at any
moment be taken in by any sort of tale; the more improbable,
indeed, the better. He makes Edmund plausible even if the

incriminating letter is not. And what better way to confirm a
nervous, puzzled, opinionated man in an error than to reason
calmly with him against it? Your victim will instinctively take
the opposite point of view and forget that this was yours to begin
with.[27] Does not the credulous nature crave to be deceived? Moreover, Shakespeare's first concern is to develop character, to put us
on terms with these people; not till that is done, he knows, will
their doings and sufferings really affect us. So it suits him, in any
case, to subordinate, for a little, what they do to what they are.
And we part from Gloucester in this scene knowing him for a
start pretty well.

The sensual man does not stand up very resolutely against
blows dealt to his complacent affections. Disillusion leaves Gloucester not only wax in Edmund's hands but more helpless than it
belongs to him to be—fair-weather sailor though he has ever
been!—in the alien troubles that now center round him. Shakespeare's maneuvering of him through these scenes—from the
welcome to the "noble arch and patron" to the moment when his
guest's honored fingers are plucking at his eyes—is a good example of the fruitful economy with which, once a character has
"come alive," its simplest gesture, its very muteness is made significant. And Gloucester has been alive from the beginning; no
illustration for a thesis, but unself-consciously himself. This very
unself-consciousness is turned later to tragic account. Fate's worst
revenge on him is that, blinded, he comes to see himself so clearly
as he is, and to find the world, which once went so comfortably
with him, a moral chaos. We might wonder at the amount of
agonized reflection in this kind allotted to him. But mark its
culmination:

[27] But it follows that upon these lines we cannot be brought to a very close
knowledge of Edgar too. Give him the same scope, and he must either get on the
track of the truth or prove himself as great a fool as his father. So Shakespeare,
now and at his next appearance, does as little with him as possible. This delays
—and dangerously—our gaining interest in him. But a play survives sins of
omission when the smallest sin of commission may damn it. Besides, time is
valuable; and a subplot cannot, for the moment, be spared much more. The likeli-
hood of the detail of this traffic between father and sons, the sending of letters, the
"retire with me to my lodging . . . there's my key" and the rest, depends somewhat upon the large, loose organization of a great nobleman's household of that
day, of which Shakespeare's audience would know well enough.

> The king is mad: how stiff is my vile sense
> That I stand up, and have ingenious feeling
> Of my huge sorrows! Better I were distract:
> So should my thoughts be sever'd from my griefs,
> And woes by wrong imaginations lose
> The knowledge of themselves.

The one thing, it seems, that the average sensual man cannot endure is knowledge of the truth. Better death or madness than that!

Yet which of us must not feelingly protest that the Gloucester, who threads and fumbles his way so well-meaningly about the family battlefield his house is turned into (much against his will), is very harshly used indeed? Is this poetic justice? He does all that one who respects his superiors may do to save Kent from the ignominy of the stocks. He does his best to pacify Lear.

> I would have all well betwixt you.

How familiar is that heartfelt cry of the man who sees no sense in a quarrel! When he does take sides his reasons and his method are not heroic, it is true.

> These injuries the king now bears will be revenged home; there is part of a power already footed; we must incline to the king. I will look to him and privily relieve him, go you and maintain talk with the duke, that my charity be not of him perceived. If he asks for me, I am ill and gone to bed.

No, truly, it is not heroic, when battle is joined, to be ill and go to bed. But caution is a sort of a virtue; and the keeping of a family foot in each camp has good sanction. Yet who can be altogether wise? In his next breath comes

> If I die for it, as no less is threatened me, the king, my old master, must be relieved.

And this his best impulse is his undoing. Unwittingly he is telling Edmund how best to betray him. He points the way; Edmund has but to follow it—just a little further. Irony deepens when later he calls upon Cornwall to spare him in the sacred name of that hospitality which, towards his king, he himself has so spinelessly betrayed. Yet, "tied to the stake," he can "stand the course" courageously enough; and he recovers self-respect in hopeless defiance of his tyrants. With just a little luck he need never have lost it. Now he is blinded and turned helpless from his own doors. Is this poetic justice upon a gentleman, whose worst fault has been to play for safety, his worst blunder to think ill of a man without question and to believe a liar? Disquieting to think that it may be![28]

Edmund is, in wickedness, half-brother to Iago. Having no such great nature as Othello's to work on, Shakespeare has no need of such transcendent villainy; and he lessens and vulgarizes his man by giving him one of those excuses for foul play against the world which a knave likes to find as a point of departure. His first soliloquy is a complete enough disclosure. The fine flourish of

> Thou, Nature, art my goddess . . . .

(finer by its surprise for us in the mouth of the modest young man of the earlier scene), and the magnificent rejection of conventional morality narrow to their objective in

> Well, then,
> Legitimate Edgar, I must have your land.

And from this firm businesslike basis Edmund, except for pure pose, never soars again. The later

> This is the excellent foppery of the world . . . .

is enjoyable argument doubtless, and doubtless he chuckles over it. There is a sporting and imaginative touch, perhaps, in the trick that finally gets rid of Edgar; the stabbing his own arm, we feel, is to his credit. But for the rest, a strict attention to business, and a quick eye to one main chance after the other, suffice him. And this, really, is almost the loathliest thing about the man. He not only betrays his father to Cornwall, but he cants about loyalty the while. He accepts the attentions of Regan and Goneril without surprise or embarrassment (he is a handsome young fellow and he knows it), calculates which will be the more desirable connection, but will leave Goneril to get rid of her husband alone

---

[28] For an earlier stroke of irony—only to be fully appreciated perhaps by the shade of Lady Gloucester—consider the exclamation wrung from the distracted old man at the climax of his wrath against Edgar:

> O strong and fasten'd villain!
> Would he deny his letter? *I never got him.*

And this to Edmund his bastard!

if that risky task has to be undertaken. It even passes through his
mind that she herself—if not Regan—may in her turn have to be
"put away." His tardy repentance does not touch us; and he puts
it into practice too tardily.[29] The queer snobbery which prompts
him to say to the still visored Edgar

> If thou'rt noble,
> I do forgive thee.

and the still queerer vanity (at such a moment!) of

> Yet Edmund was beloved.
> The one the other poison'd for my sake,
> And after slew herself.

may strike upon some ears as all but ridiculous. He is an ignoble
scoundrel and he makes an ignoble end.

Still, his methods have been interesting. The first attack upon
his father's credulity was, as we saw, both bold and apt; and what
could be safer support to the fiction of Edgar's plot than the
counterfeit truth of

> When I dissuaded him from his intent . . .
>   he replied,
> Thou unpossessing bastard! dost thou think,
> If I would stand against thee, would the reposal
> Of any trust, virtue, or worth in thee
> Make thy words faith'd? No: what I should deny,—
> As this I would; ay, though thou didst produce
> My very character, I'd turn it all
> To thy suggestion, plot, and damned practice.

For masterly confounding of counsel this should rouse the admiration of the most practiced liar. Whether, later, there is need for
him to be so snivelingly hypocritical with Cornwall we may
question. But he is still on promotion; and that shrewd, forthright
brute, if not deceived, will be the more flattered by this tribute of
vice to his virtue.

But once he is in the saddle, and when not one royal lady, but
two, have lost their heads over him, what a change!

> Know of the duke if his last purpose hold,
> Or whether since he is advised by aught

---

[29] His "Ask me not what I know," in which he takes example from Goneril—
and Iago!—is given by one Quarto and some editors to Goneril herself, with (I
fancy) good enough reason.

To change his course; he's full of alteration
And self-reproving; bring his constant pleasure.

This he says publicly of no less a man than Albany, whom later he salutes with an ironically patronizing

Sir, you speak nobly.

He is losing his head, one fears, in the flush of his fire-new fortune. Albany, however, waits his time and prepares for it; this mild gentleman should have been better reckoned with. For, of a sudden, Edmund finds that he has climbed, even as his blinded father set out in misery to climb, to the edge of a steep. And it is an apposite phrase indeed which flashes the depths on him:

Half-blooded fellow, yes!

—from an Albany not so mild. The wheel is coming circle.

This individual catastrophe and its contriving are a good example of Shakespeare's adapting of end to means (that constant obligation of the dramatist), and of his turning disability to advantage. His very need to compress close these latter incidents of Edmund's rise to fortune helps him make it the more egregious. The fact that but a dozen speeches seem to lift the fellow towards the grasping of the very power of which Lear divested himself at the play's beginning should make our recollection of that modest young man in the background of its first scene the more amazing to us. It is, at this juncture, a breathless business for all concerned. Then at the climax comes the sudden isolation of the upstart, brave in his armor, flushed with his triumph. And Shakespeare releases the tension—and rewards himself for his economy —in the sounding of trumpets, the fine flow and color of some heroic verse quite in his old style, and all the exciting ceremony of the duel.[30] Late in the play as this comes, and of secondary concern to the greater tragedy as it may be, not a point of its thriftily developed drama must be missed.

Edgar is a "slow starter" and shows no promise at all as a hero. Not here, however, but in Shakespeare's use of him as Poor Tom will be the actor's greater handicap. For by the time he is free from

---

[30] Compare the "defiances" of this scene with the passage between Mowbray and Norfolk in the beginning of *Richard II*.

this arbitrary bondage the play has put our attention and emotions
to some strain and we are no longer so well disposed to the
development of a fresh serious interest. Otherwise there is every
dramatic fitness in his tardy coming to his own. Edmund flashes
upon us in pinchbeck brilliance; the worth of Edgar waits discovery, and trial and misfortune must help discover it—to himself
above all.

> a brother noble,
> Whose nature is so far from doing harms
> That he suspects none; on whose foolish honesty
> My practices ride easy!

says Edmund of him in proper contempt. "What are you?" asks
his unknowing father, when his fortunes are still at their worst.
And he answers:

> A most poor man, made tame to fortune's blows;
> Who, by the art of known and feeling sorrows,
> Am pregnant to good pity.

But, by the play's end, it is to him as well as to Kent that Albany
turns with

> Friends of my soul, you twain
> Rule in this realm, and the gor'd state sustain.

What are the steps by which he passes from nobody to somebody?
His very reserve at the beginning can give him a stamp of
distinction, and should be made to do so. And the notion of that
strange disguise would not come, we may say, to a commonplace
man. Through the ravings of Poor Tom we can detect something
of the mind of Edgar with its misprision of the sensual life—of
his father's life, is it? We can certainly see his pitiful heart; this
Shakespeare stresses. But only in the soliloquies that end Act III,
Scene vi, and begin Act IV do we discover the full mind of the
man[31]:

> When we our betters see bearing our woes,
> We scarcely think our miseries our foes.
> Who alone suffers, suffers most i' the mind,
> Leaving free things and happy shows behind;

---

[31] The Folio rejects the first of those two and (see p. 20, note) the producer
may be wise to.

> But then the mind much sufferance doth o'erskip,
> When grief hath mates, and bearing fellowship. . . .

and

> Yet better thus, and known to be contemn'd,
> Than still contemn'd and flatter'd. To be worst,
> The lowest and most dejected thing of fortune,
> Stands still in esperance, lives not in fear;
> The lamentable change is from the best;
> The worst returns to laughter. . . .

We seem to have found the play's philosopher. And the sententiousness of the earlier soliloquy, differing both in form and tone from anything that has preceded it in the play, is surely a deliberate contrivance to lower the tension of the action and to prepare us for the calmer atmosphere—by comparison—of the play's ending. Shakespeare may afterwards have repented of it as sounding too sententious and as coming uselessly for its wider purpose immediately before the blinding of Gloucester. But Edgar's philosophy of indifference to fortune, of patience with life itself, of the good comfort of fellowship, is now, certainly, to dominate the play. It is summed up for us more than once.

> **Bear free and patient thoughts.**

he tells his father, when, by his queer stratagem—again, it was not the notion of a commonplace mind—he has saved him from despair. His playing the peasant with the insufferable Oswald is, yet again, not commonplace; and, having killed him:

> He is dead. I am only sorry
> He had no other deathsman.[32]

To him is given the answer to Gloucester's deadly

> As flies to wanton boys, are we to the gods;
> They kill us for their sport.

in

> therefore, thou happy father,
> Think that the clearest gods, who make them honours
> Of men's impossibilities, have preserved thee.

---

[32] "Chill pick your teeth, sir," suggests that he stabs him, either with a knife he wears, or, possibly, with Oswald's own dagger, wrested after a tussle.

To him is given

> The gods are just, and of our pleasant vices
> Make instruments to plague us.

But before this, his good name and his father's death justly avenged, what is the first thing he says as he discloses himself to the doubly damned scoundrel lying at his feet?

> Let's exchange charity.

Edgar, in fact, has become a man of character indeed, modest, of a discerning mind, and, in this pagan play, a very Christian gentleman.[33]

BURGUNDY, FRANCE, ALBANY, CORNWALL

Burgundy and France hardly outpass convention, though the one gains enough character from his laconic indifference, while the spirit and quality of France's speeches should keep him a pleasant memory to the play's end.[34]

Cornwall has "character" in abundance. He and Albany stand all but mute at their first appearance.[35] But from our next sight of him to our last he justifies in action and speech Gloucester's description:

> My dear lord,
> You know the fiery quality of the duke;
> How unremoveable and fix'd he is
> To his own course.

~~~~~~~~~~

[33] He is, I think, as true a gentleman as the plays give us. And he is kept himself and no mere moralizer to the last. When Lear sinks dying, it is Edgar who starts forward to recover him, till Kent checks him with the immortal

> Vex not his ghost: O! let him pass; he hates him
> That would upon the rack of this tough world
> Stretch him out longer.

For Edgar is still very young.

[34] Here is one of the difficulties incidental to the production of such a play as *King Lear* with a company gathered in for the occasion. The quality of the actors available tends to diminish with the importance of the parts. Pay apart, an actor of authority and distinction will not attach himself to a theater for the sole purpose of playing France. Hence the need of an established company with all its compensating opportunities. France is a powerful king and Cordelia's husband; and if he does not impress us as he should, and lodge himself in our memories, not only is the play immediately the poorer, but Cordelia, returning, is robbed of a background of great importance to her.

[35] By the text of the Quarto absolutely mute.

He is a man, we may suppose, in the prime of life; old enough, at least, to say to Edmund

> thou shalt find a dearer father in my love.

He is by no means a stupid man: the cynical humor with which he appraises Kent shows that. He asserts himself against his wife as Albany does not. He can speak up to Lear when need be, but he is not too swift to do it. In his vindictiveness he still keeps his head.

> Go seek the traitor Gloucester,
> Pinion him like a thief, bring him before us.
> Though well we may not pass upon his life
> Without the form of justice, yet our power
> Shall do a courtesy to our wrath, which men
> May blame but not control.

But this hardly makes him the more likable. And though we might allow him some credit for at least doing his own dirty work, it is evident that he enjoys Gloucester's blinding, for he sets about it with a savage jest. The taste of blood seems to let loose all the wild beast in him; and, like a wild beast, Shakespeare has him dispatched. Yet Cornwall is a forceful character; and there are those who—having no more concern with them than to profit by their forcefulness—can find, strangely enough, something to admire in such men. So he may be allowed a certain dog-toothed attractiveness in performance.

Albany is at the opposite pole. He prefers a quiet life with Goneril while he can contrive to lead it, even at the cost of some self-respect.

> Striving to better, oft we mar what's well.

seems to stand as his motto; and it sounds the more sententious by its setting in a rhymed couplet. His "milky gentleness," his "harmful mildness" ring true enough as accusations: does he think to tame a tigress with a platitude? His wife, quite naturally, departs to seek Regan's help without him.

Much has happened, though, by the time we see him again, when Goneril is on the full tide of reckless triumphant wickedness. She takes no heed of Oswald's

> never man so changed . . .

still presumes on

> the cowish terror of his spirit . . .

and even, when she meets him changed indeed, is blind and deaf
to the change. That Albany had loved his wife is made plain. We
hear him speak in his quiet way of "the great love" he bore her.
He has been slow to think ill of her. But he is of those who let
their wrath gather beneath a placid surface till, on a sudden, it
boils over, and if the cause of it lies deep they are never the same
again. Shakespeare, who cannot spare much space for his development, gives us this impression of the man by allowing us chiefly
these contrasted sights of him, the long interval between. And the
first stern clash with Goneril has a double purpose and nets a
double dramatic gain. It wins Albany the authoritative standing
that he now needs in the play, and it shows us a Goneril so pos-
sessed by self-will that our own surprise at the change in him
turns to surprise that she can be so oblivious of it. We may count
her a doomed creature from this moment.

Henceforth he is pitted against Edmund; the aristocrat against
the upstart; the man with nothing to gain for himself against the
man who must win and still win or perish; the man who, to the
taunt of "moral fool," can answer

> Where I could not be honest,
> I never yet was valiant.

against the man who can tell his follower as he sends him to
commit an atrocious murder:

> know thou this, that men
> Are as the time is; to be tender-minded
> Does not become a sword; thy great employment
> Will not bear question; either say thou'lt do 't,
> Or thrive by other means.

The world's allegiance is ever swaying between such leaderships.

Albany, once in action, is as distinguished a figure as any in
the play. Shakespeare endows him with a fine sense of irony. The
slight sting in the tail of his compliment to Edmund after the
battle:

> Sir, you have showed to-day your valiant strain,
> And fortune led you well . . . .

the cutting courtesy of

> Sir, by your patience,
> I hold you but a subject of this war,
> Not as a brother.

his cool preparation of his stroke; the stroke itself:

> Stay yet, hear reason. Edmund, I arrest thee
> On capital treason; and, in thy arrest,
> This gilded serpent. For your claim, fair sister,
> I bar it in the interest of my wife;
> 'Tis she is sub-contracted to this lord,
> And I, her husband, contradict your banns.
> If you will marry, make your loves to me,
> My lady is bespoke.

—are not bad for a moral fool.

Nor does he trust to the appearance of the unknown champion for Edmund's undoing. He throws his own gauntlet down. A touch of gallantry, though Shakespeare does not—does not need to—compromise his dignity by setting him to fight. And he is left from now to the play's end in command of its action.[36]

OSWALD AND THE MINOR PARTS

A modern audience must lose almost as much of the flavor of Oswald as of the Fool; and more still must be lost if he is stripped of his doublet and hose, forbidden his swagger and his curtseys and thrust back into the dark ages. We cannot be expected to cheer—as I doubt not Shakespeare's audience did—when Kent breaks out with

> That such a slave as this should wear a sword,
> Who wears no honesty!

nor to take the precise point of Lear's

> How now, where's that mongrel?

that newfàngled fellow, neither gentleman nor plain servant, mimicking the manners of the one, doing dirtier work than the other. Kent sizes him up when he dresses him down, with enjoyable completeness; so does Lear, later, in a dozen words:

---

[36] Though the last speech should possibly, in accordance with the Folio, be Edgar's.

> This is a slave, whose easy-borrowed pride
> Dwells in the fickle grace of her he follows.

So does Edgar, having rid the world of him, as

> a serviceable villain;
> As duteous to the vices of thy mistress
> As badness would desire.

Oswalds have existed in every age and been good game for abuse, but the London of Shakespeare's day had evidently produced an unusually fine crop of them. His own sayings are colorless compared with what is said of him. It follows, then, that his "Ay, madams" and "No, madams," his "I'll not be strucken, my lord," his "Prithee, if thou lovest me, tell me," and his "Out, dunghill," when the peasant's cudgel threatens to knock his dishonorable sword out of his hand, must answer exactly in accent and attitude, as he himself in look and manner, to the very sort of being Shakespeare had in mind. In himself he is nothing; a "whoreson zed," an "unnecessary letter," and he should seem no more. But, as a tailor made him, he must be tailored right.

It remains to notice one or two of Shakespeare's minuter touches. When Gloucester has been blinded, branded a traitor and turned from his own house to smell his way to Dover, he finds one fearless friend; the old peasant who has been his tenant and his father's tenant "these fourscore years." The savagery of the blinding itself had stirred one common fellow to risk and lose his life stopping the worst of it. Two other common fellows have the charity to bind up the wounds; but they'll risk no more than that. The old peasant, too old himself to go far with his lord, shakes a sad head at leaving him in such company as Poor Tom, and will risk his fortunes to do Gloucester, in his ruin and disgrace, a last simple service. Close following the transcendent scenes of Lear's madness and the extreme brutality of the blinding comes this interlude of servant and peasant, of common humanity in its bravery and charity with its simple stumbling talk. The whole effect is made in a dozen lines or so, but gains importance by its homespun contrast and by its placing across the main dividing line of the play's action.

And for a happy instance of Shakespeare's power to suggest a

man in a dozen words, take the reply of the Captain to whom
Edmund confides the murder of Lear and Cordelia:

> I cannot draw a cart nor eat dried oats;
> If it be man's work, I'll do it.

Staging and Costume

No more need be urged, I hope, against a realistic staging of the
play or anything approaching one. But whether the single alternative to this is the actuality of Shakespeare's own theater is
another question, which the producer must answer for himself. If
he protests that his audience will never sit so unconsciously before
a reproduction of the Globe stage as did Shakespeare's before the
thing itself one cannot contradict him. But he cuts from the
anchorage at his peril. And the doubt is as to whether when he
has found some, presumably, atmospheric sort of background,
which does not positively conflict with the play's stagecraft, the
result—for all its visual beauty—will be worth the risk and the
trouble.

Abide by Shakespeare's own stage, and no questions of importance arise upon the use of it. But for Edgar's moment "above,"
some need for the masking of Lear's "state," and again for the
discovery of the joint-stools and bench in the scene of the mock
trial, the play could indeed be acted upon a barer stage than was
the Globe's.[87] The great chair with the unconscious Lear in it
may be more conveniently carried from an inner stage, and Poor
Tom will emerge more effectively from one than from a sidedoor.
But this is all; and it may even be that Shakespeare minimized
such localization as his theater did afford him to give the play
spaciousness of action, and to magnify his characters the more in
isolating them from needless detail of circumstance. Let the
producer, at any rate—and at all costs—provide for the action's
swift unencumbered movement and for our concentration upon
the characters themselves, in whom everything is concentrated.

As for costume, this is one of the few plays in which Shakespeare took some trouble to do more than its subject itself would

---

[87] There are one or two signs that the stage to which the Folio version was
fitted differed a little from that of the Quarto.

do to dissociate it from his own time; though even so he will not have relied overmuch upon costume to help him. But only here and there is his own seventeenth century patent, and that in character or incident of minor importance. The prevailing atmosphere and accent is barbaric and remote. Edmund's relationship to Iago may seem to us to give him a certain Italianate flavor, and Edgar's beginning suggests bookishness and the Renaissance. But clothe these two as we please, their substance will defy disguise. Oswald, as we have argued, is a topical picture; in the Ancient Briton he will be all but obliterated. That must be faced. Of the Fool, by shifting him back a dozen centuries, we lose little, because, as we have argued, we are bound already to lose so much. And if a Fool in a barbarous king's retinue seems to us an anachronism (though it may be doubted if—for all the preciseness that would take offense at a Henry V in doublet and hose—it will), the fantasy of the part marks it out as the fittest note of relief from consistency. To consistency in such matters no dated play of Shakespeare can be submitted. Here our main losses by desertion of seventeenth century habit and manners will end. And such anachronism as may lie in Cordelia's chance of being Duchess of Burgundy, in "base foot-ball player" and "unfee'd lawyer," in the stocks, some of Poor Tom's talk and Lear's ravings, and in the procedure of the challenge and the duel, will be inconsiderable however the characters are clothed.

So a producer is free to balance these items against an imagined Britain, whose king swears

> by the mysteries of Hecate and the night . . .

(not to mention Apollo), and where a Duke of Cornwall turns public executioner. There is no doubt, I think, in which scale advantage lies. The play should be costumed according to the temper that Shakespeare has given it, a splendid barbaric temper. It is equally clear that archaeological accuracy profits nothing. Nor should the producer lose more than he need of such sophistication as Shakespeare himself retained.

The Music

ABOUT the music there is little to be said. I do not imagine much improvement possible upon "the consort of viols," to the quiet harmonies of which Lear was meant, one presumes, to be waked. The sennet that announces his first regal appearance should be noted, as well as the flourish to herald France and Burgundy, and the ceremonial difference between the two. The *Horns within*, which prelude Lear's return from hunting, ask no comment. A trumpet is used with dramatic effect before Cornwall's entrance in Act II, Scene i; it reinforces Gloucester's excitement. The same sound stirs Lear a little later and strings him up for the encounter with Goneril. And, towards the play's end, the triple sounding by the herald, to be answered, when our suspense is keenest, by Edgar's trumpet without, is a most carefully calculated dramatic effect.[88] We have noticed earlier how the battle in which Cordelia's forces are defeated is dramatically minimized; its musical symbolism consists only of an alarum and an alarum and retreat. But the *Drum afar off*, to the ominous sound of which the longest and most varied scene of the fourth act closes, has very definite value. So has the dead march with which the play itself ends.

The Fool is allotted no formal and completed song, but, needless to say, his snatches of melody should be melodious indeed. This musical and lyrical relief to the strain of Lear's passion is, as we have argued elsewhere, an essential part of the play's stagecraft. The technique of the singing should not be artificial; rather that of an accomplished folk-song singer. And where no authentically traditional tunes exist, folk music will prove a sufficient quarry.

The Text

THE complications of the text are troublesome. Corruptions, obvious and suspected, apart, the producer is confronted by the problem of the three hundred lines, or nearly, that the Quartos give and the Folio omits, and of the hundred given by the Folio and omitted from the Quartos. Editors, considering only, it would seem, that the more Shakespeare we get the better, bring practi-

---

[88] Beethoven found a similar one useful in *Fidelio*.

cally the whole lot into the play we read. But a producer must ask himself whether these two versions do not come from different prompt books, and whether the Folio does not, both in cuts and additions, sometimes represent Shakespeare's own second thoughts. In general, surely, the Folio is of better authority; it is at least more carefully transcribed. Some of its cuts are of passages which seem to have been found constructionally unnecessary. Some only "ease" the dialogue; they are of varying importance and aptness. Where Quarto and Folio offer alternatives, to adopt both versions may make for redundancy or confusion.[39]

To deal with the major differences. In the scene of the dividing of the kingdom the Folio's stressed identification of Albany and Cornwall, France and Burgundy, seems deliberate and is certainly valuable. Of the additions to the Gloucester-Edmund-Edgar scene the same may be said. Gloucester can hardly be shown too distracted, and the hiding-away of Edgar from his father is a good point made. But, in compensation, the Folio cuts the mockery of Gloucester's foibles with which Edmund preludes his attempt on Edgar's confidence—and one sees why.

In Goneril's first scene with Oswald the Folio's omissions save some repetition and show her to us terser and less familiar with her servant. A Folio cut in the Fool's part a little later—his rhyming upon the "sweet and bitter fool," and the joke about monopolizing—may seem at a first glance a little clumsy. But we shall hardly appreciate the gibe at monopolies unless we rewrite it "trusts"; probably the Quarto's audiences had appreciated it too well. The whole cut is a useful tightening of the dialogue. Yet a little later the Folio gives us (as the Quarto does not) a passage in which Goneril justifies herself to Albany; undoubtedly useful.

When Lear finds Kent in the stocks and has listened in silence to the story of his being set there, by the Quarto

O, how this mother swells up toward my heart . . . .

follows immediately upon Kent's story. The Folio gives the Fool a little piping song, while Lear still stands speechless, his agony upon him. The dramatic effect will be appreciably different.

---

[39] I speak from now on of "the Quarto" because for the purposes of this argument the "Pied Bull" and "Butter" Quartos might be one.

Later the Folio alone gives us a passage in which Regan justifies Goneril.

In Act III, Scene i, the Folio cuts some important lines out of the Gentleman's second speech. In particular

> Strives in his little world of man to outscorn
> The to-and-fro-conflicting wind and rain.

has vanished. An inefficient actor might have been the cause of this. A few lines later Folio and Quarto offer us alternative cuts. That of the Folio is perhaps the clumsier of the two. It stresses the call for Cordelia's help but barely hints at her army's landing, which the Quarto emphasizes. We may or may not have here the cutting of a common original (of which still more may have existed; for of the

> servants, who seem no less,
> Which are to France the spies and speculations
> Intelligent of our state . . .

we do not hear again). The object of the cut in both cases—and possibly the cutting of the Gentleman's speech also—is evidently to shorten this prelude to Lear's great entrance. What should a producer do here? Shakespeare leaves us to the end a little unconvinced by the machinery of Cordelia's return. There is no dramatic profit in the confusion. Neither text may be as Shakespeare left it. But in this instance I prefer the Quarto's to an amalgam of the two.

Of Merlin's prophecy I have spoken elsewhere.[40]

Let us in passing note the Folio's most important addition of two lines' preparation for the critical

> Poor naked wretches, wheresoe'er you are . . .

In them the kindness to the half-drowned Fool is emphasized; and he is (I think) sent off the stage so that there may be no danger whatever of discord or incongruity. The actor of the Fool, possibly, was never quite to be relied on; and even if he could be, there was always the chance that some buffoon in the audience would vent an incongruous guffaw at the mere sight of him sitting there. But, above all, by these two lines the meaning and intention of what is to come are emphasized:

---

[40] p. 58.

In, boy; go first. You houseless poverty—
Nay, get thee in. *I'll pray, and then I'll sleep.*

I italicize the vitally important phrase. It is dangerous to dogmatize; but this addition has to me all the air of being a second thought of Shakespeare's own.

We come to the Folio's omission of the mock trial. Time may, as we said, have demanded some omissions, and this scene may have been chosen rather than something better liked by the actors or (seemingly) audience. It can hardly have proved ineffective, technically "daring" though it is. It certainly does not today; and very certainly one cannot imagine Shakespeare regretting he had written it.

The cut at the end of this scene, however, asks more consideration; for a purely dramatic reason can be found for the omission of Edgar's soliloquy. It must lower the tension of the action. This may damage the scene of Gloucester's blinding, which follows immediately; and if an act-pause is to follow, the tension will, of course, be lowered then. The chief purpose of the soliloquy, moreover, is to give Edgar a fresh start in his dramatic career. It is a quiet start, the effect of which the violent scene that follows must do much to obliterate. When the Folio, then, postpones it to the beginning of Act IV, it does Edgar a double service, as the Quarto doubles the disservice by making the second soliloquy, when it comes, seem dramatically redundant. Without hesitation, I should here follow the Folio text. The further cutting of Kent's lines, however,

Oppressed nature sleeps . . .

is probably due to a quick closing of the inner stage, which may have obviated the lifting of the sleeping Lear, and it has not the same validity.

The Folio also cuts the significant piece of dialogue between the two servants with which the third act ends. I cannot pretend to say why, if it was not that when this text was settled, the actors to speak the lines were lacking. No one need abide by this cut.

The disappearance of Edgar's "Obidicut, Hobbididance" and the rest from the first scene with his father is, I think, to the good. A few lines before he says:

I cannot daub it further.

And in any case the effect of the mad lingo will have been exhausted in the scenes with Lear.

We next come to some ruthless cutting of Albany by the Folio. Shakespeare may have yielded here to the exigencies of bad acting or to a wish to knit the action more closely. But he is taking some pains at this juncture to develop Albany, and we shall be on the safe side in keeping to the fuller text.

Now, however, the Folio omits one entire scene. It is a carpentered scene if ever there was one. It begins with a lame explanation of the nonappearance of the King of France; it goes on to a preparation for the reappearance of Cordelia and it ends with some unconvincing talk about Lear's "burning shame" and Kent's disguise. I could better believe that Shakespeare cut it than wrote it. There is, certainly, a little life in the description of Cordelia, and a case can be made for so heralding her return to the play. The rest is explanation of what is better left unexplained; and whoever, between the making of the Quarto and the Folio, discovered this—Shakespeare or another—did the play a good service, which we shall wisely profit by.

The remaining differences between the two versions show, in the Folio, a further cutting of explanatory stuff, by which we may well abide; a certain slicing into Albany and Edmund that neither hurts them much now, nor, it is true, does much to spur the action; the loss of one or two lines (Cordelia's in particular) that we shall not want to lose, and the gain of a few that seem good second thoughts. There are, besides, one or two changes that seem merely to reflect change in stage practice as between Quarto and Folio.

On the whole, then—and if he show a courageous discretion—I recommend a producer to found himself on the Folio. For that it does show some at least of Shakespeare's own reshapings I feel sure.

Among other slightly vexed questions, the following are particularly worth attention (the lineal references are to the [English] Arden Shakespeare).

Act I, Scene i, 35. There is no authority for Edmund's exit, and the producer is quite at liberty to let him stay and listen to the momentous proceedings.

Scene v, 1. I give a guess that "Gloucester" in this line is a slip
for "Cornwall." There is no other evidence that Lear writes
to the Earl of Gloucester, nor any reason he should, nor any
evidence at all that Cornwall lived near the town.

52-3. This couplet has the sanction (as Merlin's prophecy has not)
of both Quarto and Folio. But I find its authenticity hard to
credit. Shakespeare could write bawdry, and sometimes at
what seem to us the unlikeliest moments. This does not
smack of the Fool, though, or of what Shakespeare wants
of him.

Act II, Scene i, 20. *Enter Edgar*. This stage direction is wrongly placed
—and typically—in modern editions. The Quarto places it
four lines, the Folio a line, earlier. Even the Folio, then,
shows that he enters on the upper stage and is visible to the
audience before Edmund sees him. It may seem a small matter, but the difference between an independent entrance and
being called on like a dog is appreciable, and can affect a
character's importance. Edgar does descend, of course.

Scene ii, 168-73. "Nothing almost sees miracles, But misery . . .
and shall find time From this enormous state, seeking to give
Losses their remedies." Cut this much, and an actor can make
sense of a passage otherwise as obscure as it is evidently
corrupt.

Scene iii. I think, on the whole, that there is no scene-division
here; there is not, that is to say, a cleared stage. Curtains
might be drawn before Kent in the stocks, but he may as
well sit there asleep while Edgar soliloquizes. On an *unlocalized* stage I doubt its puzzling even a modern audience if
he does; it certainly would not have troubled Shakespeare's.

Act III, Scene iii. The Quarto stage-direction *Enter . . . with lights*
shows, I think, if nothing else does, the use of the inner stage
for this scene.

Scene vii, 23. Neither Quarto nor Folio specifies Oswald's exit,
and they get Edmund's and Goneril's wrong. But it is plain
that Oswald should be gone immediately on the command to
get horses for his mistress. Edmund's and Goneril's leave-
taking then stands out the plainer, and the "strange œilliads
and most speaking looks" that pass between them as they
go may be made noticeable to Regan—and to us.

Act IV, Scene iv, 6. "Centurie" says the Quarto and "centery" the
Folio; and this surely will be understood even now (and
whatever the anachronism) to mean a hundred men. Why

send one sentry to look for Lear? And why a sentry, any how?

Act V, Scene iii, 161. "Ask me not what I know." The Quarto gives this to Goneril and marks her exit accordingly. It is at least a question whether the Folio's change is not erroneous. For Edmund's so sudden change of front is not easily explicable.

284. This is the first and only indication that Kent's name in disguise has been "Caius." I cannot discover that any editor has commented upon the strangeness of Kent—Kent of all people, and at this moment of all others—asking Lear, apparently, a kind of conundrum. The Pied Bull Quarto at least gives no note of interrogation. If the line can be spoken as if it meant

Your servant Kent, who was your servant Caius . . .

it will at least not be confusing. Can it not, perhaps, be so read? Kent in his next line plainly appropriates the question to himself.

324. The Quarto gives the last speech to Albany, the Folio to Edgar. Convention would allot it to Albany as the man of rank. "We that are young" sounds more like Edgar. But remembering how much Albany's part is cut in the Folio, it is likely, I think, that this change to Edgar was deliberately made, and therefore it should stand.

1927; PARTLY REVISED in 1935

Macbeth

To pitch upon an informing epithet, *Macbeth* is the starkest of the great tragedies. It is the least discursive, even less so than *Othello*. With *Othello* it is the most forthright in its action; and this we should expect, for it is the tragedy of unchecked will, even as *Hamlet* is the tragedy of indecision. It is cold and harsh and unrelenting. If Shakespeare's mind was ever plagued by the doctrine of hell hereafter, this play might well be his comment on it. He puts hell here. Macbeth the man is a study in self-damnation. 'Hell is murky,' says the wretched woman in her sleep, and she may have further yet to go on to find it. But he ends as a soulless man, a beast, chained to a stake and slaughtered like a beast.

So much, if it be allowed, for general guidance in picturing the play.

The Text

We meet at once with an unusual difficulty. For long, producers of the plays have been mercilessly hacking at Shakespeare's authentic work, though the custom at last is losing credit. But in *Macbeth*, however conscientious we may be, there will be forced on us, apparently, work which is not his at all.

Hecate may be ruled out with hardly a second thought. If this be not true Middleton, it is at least true twaddle, and Shakespeare – though he had his lapses – was not in a twaddling mood when he wrote *Macbeth*.

The chief difficulty is with the play's opening. Good opinion holds that we do not meet Shakespeare's true text till Macbeth's own entrance with

> So foul and fair a day I have not seen.

If this be so, should the producer boldly begin here? It will make an interesting and very possible, and indeed a most dramatic, beginning. It will be in line with the forthrightness of the play's whole action. We should have this significant note struck at once by the protagonist; the weird sisters would suddenly and silently appear, as unexpectedly to us as to him, and the main theme would be opened with dignity and directness. The experiment might be well worth trying. But, almost certainly, this was not Shakespeare's beginning. Precedent is against it. The technique of *Richard II* and *Richard III* was far behind him; and, even though in the late-written *Antony and Cleopatra* there are but ten lines to be spoken before the chief characters appear, the difference between this and the speaking of the very first word of the play is, in theatrical effect, a great one.

On the other hand it is hardly more likely that he began with the witches.[1] Apart from such an opening being un-Shakespearean, the lines themselves are as little like Shakespeare as Hecate is, and have indeed all the tang of the Hecate lines. Critical glorification of the scene and its supposed purpose has not, of course, been wanting. But this mainly belongs to the class of commentary that deals with Norns and Shakespeare's knowledge of Northern mythology and the like, and need not trouble the simple theatrical mind, to whom a play must be first and even last a play. The scene – as better and sterner critical authority allows – is a poor scene and a pointless scene. And Shakespeare did not, at any rate, begin his plays with super-

---

[1] Incidentally it must be noted that in the text they are never referred to as witches, but always as the Weird Sisters. For witches the stage directions in the Folio are alone responsible. To these – with a text so extensively corrupted – it is difficult to assign consistent value. Where they pertain to the corrupted parts the balance of probability is that they are never Shakesperean. Otherwise they may be good evidence of the traditional staging of the play, but that will be the limit of their authority. The intrinsic evidence upon this question I deal with later. (Granville-Barker's note)

fluities. For all the offence to stage tradition, therefore, it may well be omitted.

Now comes the question of Scene ii. This, we may hazard, does at least stand for Shakespeare's beginning. That the lines themselves have been mauled is obvious, whether by Middleton, some stage manager, or the compositor. There is possibly matter missing. Even allowing for some desired effect of the confusion of battle and rebellion, the scene has not that expository clearness which is one of the hall-marks of true Shakespeare.[2] As Shakespeare wrote it, probably it was a better scene. But if, as we have it, it represents something of his intention, the safe plan is perhaps to take it as the play's beginning. It at least makes a fair start.

---

[2] The difficulty about the Thane of Cawdor can indeed be overcome by assuming that Macbeth is not 'Bellona's bridegroom.' Why must we suppose he is? For one thing, if the same battle is referred to, there would be little dramatic point in Duncan's question to Rosse,

> Whence cam'st thou, worthy thane?

and the answer

> From Fife, great king.

Certainly the duplication of 'Norweyan' is confusing. But are not these the facts? 'The merciless Macdonwald,' joined with a 'Norweyan lord,' was beaten by Macbeth and Banquo. Norway himself and the Thane of Cawdor were beaten by some other general. Even so it is strange that Angus should say questioningly of Cawdor,

> . . . Whether he was combin'd
> With those of Norway, or did line the rebel
> With hidden help and vantage, or that with both
> He labour'd in his country's wrack, I know not.

Shakespeare was not apt to leave things in such a muddle at the beginning of a play.

And all this does not, of course, exhaust the difficulties of the first four scenes as they appear in the Folio. The Macbeth-Duncan meeting is unsatisfactory. Moreover – and more importantly – the disclosure of Macbeth's mind, not in a soliloquy, but in two rather ineptly contrived asides, is surely, in such a play and with such a character, un-Shakespearean.

Even if – as some critics suppose – the explanation was that he hurriedly compressed an elaborately planned opening in order to arrive more swiftly at Duncan's murder, we should still expect to find the work more skilfully done. Here is a fantastic guess; but it might really be that when it came to printing the Folio the manuscript of the first four scenes – of Middleton's revision even – had vanished, and that what we have is the result of the mobilising of memories of actors and prompter. Some lines they recalled accurately, some they confused, and some they had forgotten altogether. (Granville-Barker's note)

As to Scene iii Shakespeare may well have begun it with the weird sisters. But the present opening seems spurious, and it is quite out of key with the more authentic part of the scene. There is much to be said for boldly omitting it, and beginning, as aforesaid, with the entrance of Macbeth and Banquo.

This will dispose of the more serious textual difficulties. The porter's scene, both on the count of stagecraft[3] and on the aesthetic count, is surely genuine, and we have hardly sufficient cause to discard lines 37–59 of the scene between Lady Macduff and the child, though one must own to a suspicion of them.[4]

The entrance (Act IV, Scene iii) of the English doctor and the speech about the King's Evil is another matter. No doubt this is Shakespeare's work. It is equally obvious that he wrote it to please King James I, whom neither he nor we can any longer hope to please. But, upon kindred grounds, too much slashing may be done, and has been done. We must bring to the seeing of Shakespeare a certain historical sense. Besides, the episode has its dramatic value too. It helps to create – and there is little to do this – the benevolent atmosphere of the English court for a contrast with the description of Scotland in her agony. Certainly these twenty-two lines should be retained.

Staging and Directing

Upon a stage of typical Elizabethan equipment no difficulty of presentation need, of course, occur. And indications for the use of outer, inner and upper stage – though arguable occasionally – are not on the whole hard to follow. Until we reach

Enter Macbeth's wife alone with a letter,

the action is well enough suited to the outer stage. The weird sisters, at the Globe, *may* have appeared in the gallery. But Macbeth's 'Into the air' when they vanish, is no stronger evidence of this than is Banquo's 'The earth hath bubbles' that

---

[3] Macbeth must have time to get on his nightgown and wash his hands. (Granville-Barker's note)

[4] They show distinct signs of being an interpolation, but it does not follow they are Middleton's. Shakespeare himself might have found good reason for lengthening the scene in a wish to give greater importance to the two characters. See infra. (Granville-Barker's note)

they appeared on the ground. The dramatic effect, though, will surely be greater if they do actually stop the way upon that imaginary blasted heath.

Duncan's second scene could conceivably employ the inner stage; but then Lady Macbeth's first scene must be played above; and this seems, on the whole, an unlikely arrangement; — though a certain effect would then be gained by her descent later to welcome Duncan. But her first talk with Macbeth is an intimate one, and that argues rather the use of the inner stage.

Act I, Scene vii, might well be played on the outer stage; the procession of the

> *Sewer and divers servants with dishes and service*

sufficing to mark passage of time and change of place. Still — the chamber where Duncan was supping being thought of as below — an effect could be gained by the drawing back of the inner stage curtains and the use by Macbeth and Lady Macbeth of the actual door of the inner stage as the chamber door. This would somewhat confine their scene together, perhaps to its advantage, and would also allow the lapse of time before Act II to be emphasised by the redrawing of the curtains.

Then for Act II the outer and — as I shall suggest — the upper stages will suffice. Macbeth's 'As I descended' is evidence that Duncan's sleeping chamber is imagined above. If we presume the curtains of an inner upper stage to be drawn close, there is no need for actual going up and down during the murder, and Lady Macbeth's quick re-entrance after her exit with the daggers would not be delayed. But it will be noticed that between Macduff's

> I'll make so bold to call

and his re-entrance after the discovery twelve lines are spoken. This presumably leaves ample time for him to mount to the upper stage. Moreover, the effect of his re-entrance through the closed curtains and of his delivering,

> O horror! horror! horror!

from the gallery will be very striking. The other characters would then assemble there, and there the rest of the scene would be played. One may suggest that what Shakespeare visualised was a number of people rushing out on the landing at the sound of the alarm bell, as they would in any country house to-day. They should be more or less in their night attire. This is connoted by

> And when we have our naked frailties hid;

and

> Let's briefly put on manly readiness
> And meet i' the hall together,

is fully pointed by situating the scene thus. It would be possible too – and effective – for Malcolm and Donalbain after

> Let's away; our tears are not yet brew'd,

to descend to the lower stage and finish the scene there. The last three speeches would then seem, as they should, a postscript to the rest, rather than an anti-climax.

Act III, Scene i, seems planned for the outer stage. Scene ii could be played there as well, but it might be more effective on the inner stage. The stage-manager's difficulty would lie in the setting of the banquet for Scene iv. But this should not trouble him. And unless there is to be a long pause before Act IV (and it should be noted that the scene between Lenox and another lord obviates any) he would have to be about as quick in clearing it away and setting the cauldron for the weird sisters. Scenes iii and vi are on the outer stage, of course. And for Scene iv the outer and inner stages are used together. Scene v is to be counted apocryphal.

The arrangement for Act IV is obvious; an inner scene and two outer scenes to follow.

In Act v the direct alternation of inner and outer scenes is arguably complete. But the stage directions for Scene vii suggest that, by the time of their insertion, at any rate, some more complex arrangement had been devised. Young Siward is slain, but there is no apparent provision for removing the body.[5]

---

[5] It cannot remain to the play's end. What is to hide it from Malcolm and Siward? (Granville-Barker's note)

There is also the direction for Macbeth and Macduff,

Exeunt fighting. Alarums.

and immediately,

Enter fighting and Macbeth slain.

Then, without a pause, and, again with no provision for the removal of the body,

Retreat, flourish. Enter with drum and colours Malcolm . . .

And twenty-four lines later comes,

Enter Macduff with Macbeth's head.

We may be fairly certain that the play is meant to end on the lower stage. If Macduff and Macbeth are to have a good fight, this – or at least the best part of it – should take place on the lower stage too. Now the double stage direction will be made clear if they can leave the lower stage fighting, and re-appear in the gallery.[6] If Macbeth is killed on the inner upper stage the drawing of its curtain would conceal his body. And if young Siward had been killed there too, there would be no pressing necessity for the removal of his. If then we may imagine, besides, the curtains of the inner lower stage drawn back and both outer and inner stages in use, the directions for the whole scene could read thus:

Alarums. Enter Macbeth above.

MACBETH. They have tied me to a stake; I cannot fly . . .

Enter young Siward; either directly on the upper stage,
or by crossing the lower stage from (say) the left door.[7]

Alarums. Enter Macduff below by left door.

MACDUFF. That way the noise is . . .

Exit by right door . . .

---

[6] This would involve a momentarily empty stage, but the pause would be filled by alarums. It is a question, of course, how easily accessible the gallery at the Globe was from the lower stage. (Granville-Barker's note)

[7] Or the dialogue to the fight might even be spoken from the lower to the upper stage. (Granville-Barker's note)

Enter Malcolm and old Siward below by left door.

SIWARD. Enter, sir, the castle.

Exeunt through inner stage.

Alarum. Enter Macbeth below by right door.

MACBETH. Why should I play the Roman fool . . .

Enter Macduff below by right door. . . .

Exuent fighting, either by right door, or, possibly, through inner stage. Alarums. Re-enter fighting on upper stage. Retreat. Flourish. Enter Malcolm, etc., in procession through inner stage.

This scheme would further suggest that Scene v might be played on the upper stage. The opening line

Hang out our banners on the outward walls,

gives some colour to the idea. But it is not a scene wholly of action. It contains the more or less reflective

To-morrow, and to-morrow, and to-morrow;[8]

and much would depend upon the immediacy of touch with the audience that such a position gave to the actor. That again would largely depend upon particularities of the theatre's construction. This is the sort of consideration that must often have ruled in or out the employment of the upper stage.

With regard to any scheme of staging other than the Elizabethan one can here but elaborate a little the general principles laid down already for a more liberal treatment of the plays. Presumably such a scheme would hang to some extent upon decorative effect. That it must never clog the action is axiomatic. As to the service it can render to this particular play; it can perhaps point the action by reinforcing the effect of swift movement through the earlier scenes of preparation and increasing tension to the murder of Duncan and its discovery.[9] It can perhaps do something to point the downward rush towards the

---

[8] But for the actor's treatment of this, see infra. (Granville-Barker's note)
[9] Though, actually, no swifter movement is well possible than that for which the Elizabethan stage provides. (Granville-Barker's note)

play's end, that counterbalances the opening rise in Macbeth's fortune. It can give us something of the barbaric grandeur with which we may suppose Macbeth would emphasise his regality. It can no doubt sharpen the contrast – though the play itself provides this by one stroke after another – between the court, the sights that the weird sisters show, the simplicity of Macduff's home, the kindly security of England and the unnatural strain of that scene of tragic twilight through which Lady Macbeth's tortured spirit drifts towards death.

It will be convenient to speak here of the act division of the play, for this is bound to affect the consideration of anything that can be called scenery. Elsewhere, in dealing with the plays generally, it has been suggested that we need not feel bound by the Folio's arbitrary division of each play into five acts, nor at any rate to the observance of an interval at the end of each. And there are some signs in this play at least that in practice this particular division was not originally observed.

The play, in the light of its story, falls into three parts. Acts I and II form the first and stand for the achievement of Macbeth's ambition. Act III, with the two first scenes of Act IV, form a second, which shows his wielding of power. From thence to the end we see the process of retribution. There are dramatic advantages in this arrangement.[10]

This first part is undeniably a unit of action; and in only one place does a halt seem to be called : at the end of Act I. Here a pause will have value, a pause, that is to say, which an audience can sit through in expectant silence. But a break in the tension, such as must be made by the usual inter-act disturbance and conversation, will be equally disastrous. What is wanted dramatically is, so to speak, a few moments' vacancy, in which the vibrations of the strenuous scene that ends with

> . . . I am settled and bend up
> Each corporal agent to this terrible feat.
> Away, and mock the time with fairest show;
> False face must hide what the false heart doth know.

---

[10] One need not spend time contending it was Shakespeare's. For is Shakespeare's discoverable? Upon what basis of dramatic advantage or practical convenience was it founded? (Granville-Barker's note)

may disperse, and the audience grow sensitive to the quiet opening of Banquo's

How goes the night, boy?

If we are to imagine that the lights of the banqueting-chamber have been visible, or any snatches of music or talk heard coming from it, a slow darkening and silencing of these might gain the effect.

The second part, again, is a dramatic unit. And, if it seems to end with a comparatively unimportant scene,[11] it must be remembered that it is the murder of Lady Macduff and his son which precipitates Macduff's vengeance. This therefore leads us directly on to the third part.

It may be said that Act IV as it stands in the Folio is a better gathering of scenes. But there is this against it. Act IV, Scene iii (between Malcolm, Macduff and Rosse), is the hardest in the play to make interesting in its entirety, and it gets its best chance by being made an opening scene. Again, the sleep-walking scene, which, if Act IV of the Folio is left intact, must begin Act V, is at a grave disadvantage so placed, with its audience quite unkeyed to its necessarily subdued tone. On the other hand, the close connection of the two has great value. The contrast between Macduff and Malcolm's manly tune and the whisperings of the doctor and the waiting gentlewoman and the slumbery agitation that follows is well worth emphasising.

Let us come back to the question of the play's decoration. The barbaric splendour of Macbeth's court! That is the dangerous sort of phrase that slips into the mind when Shakespeare sets one's imagination free. The practical danger will lie, of course, in any attempt to capitalise this imagination in such extrinsic things as scenery and clothes, lights and music. We may make for safety by confining ourselves to such use of these things as Shakespeare himself had. If this appears an ignoble timidity, we must then at least see that they do not conflict with things intrinsic to the play. This principle will not be disputed

---

11 The scene is most important, and has only come to be thought otherwise by the insistent viewing of the play as a dramatic preserve for the performances of Macbeth and Lady Macbeth. (Granville-Barker's note)

perhaps, but pitfalls in practice are many and unexpected. From some of the commonly less observed of them, however, *Macbeth* is freer than most of the plays.

The question of illusionary scenery need not be argued. Woe betide the painter upon canvas who will compete with

> This castle hath a pleasant seat; the air
> Nimbly and sweetly recommends itself
> Unto our gentle senses.
>   This guest of summer,
> The temple-haunting martlet, does approve
> By his lov'd mansionry that the heaven's breath
> Smells wooingly here; no jutty, frieze,
> Buttress, nor coign of vantage, but this bird
> Hath made his pendent bed and procreant cradle:
> Where they most breed and haunt, I have observ'd
> The air is delicate;

or with

> The west yet glimmers with some streaks of day:
> Now spurs the lated traveller apace,
> To gain the timely inn.

But if we are brought to ask, how did Shakespeare – the bare equipment of his theatre apart – visualise the setting of his play, there is evidence in the writing that his sense of period and place differed not so greatly from ours – if we are not too well informed in archaeology. He may, for instance, have passed blasted heaths between London and Stratford; and so, a very little further afield, may we. But is it the general colouring of the verse rather than any particular passages that seems to show Shakespeare's vision of a wilder country than his own; strange, yet not so strange to him that, for reasons of practical artistry, the difference was better ignored. Much of this verse-colouring no doubt concerns the characters more than their habitat. Even so, there is still an overplus for the broader effect.

That Shakespeare imagined – and that his actors wore – an unusual costume is shown by Malcolm's line upon Rosse's approach,

> My countryman; but yet I know him not.

Rosse may actually have worn nothing more symbolic of Scotland than a bonnet and a claymore, but the admission is enough.

Press too far on this path, though, and the pitfalls begin. Macbeth's castle, as we have seen, had the conveniences of the Globe Theatre; and the further suggestions of the night of the murder are rather of houses and habits familiar to that audience than of Scotland in the year A.D. 1000. Bells ring, people get on their nightgowns,[12] and the porter makes topical jokes. And though in the matter of costume we have neither Cleopatra's 'Cut my lace, Charmian,' to contend with, nor the subtler incongruities which crop out when we try to present the Italianate Claudius of Denmark as half a Viking, or Cloten, the player at bowls and provider of serenades, as an ancient Briton, in *Macbeth*, too, archaeology will insensibly undo us.

The decorator, then, of this particular tragedy may count himself lucky to be as untrammelled as he is, and so little plagued by such anachronisms (mostly of the modern mind's creating) as cripple an interpretation of the more strictly historical plays. Let him strike, may we suggest, an agreement with producer and actors upon the mood of the play, and help to project *that* into its environing and equipment; as, within these covers, Mr Charles Ricketts has now alone so admirably done.[13]

Music

Little enough use is, or well can be, made of music. There are few plays of Shakespeare in which this amenity – and all other such – is so sternly repressed. Hence, no doubt, Middleton's incursion with his songs and dances. It looks, however, as if the twice repeated inclusion of 'Ho-boyes' in the directions for Duncan's arrival at Inverness might be Shakespearean enough, and may indicate a festivity of welcome.[14] If so, it is just such a good stroke of irony as we should expect. The second direction may also indicate music during the banquet. It

---

[12] An Elizabethan nightgown, needless to say, was more a dressing-gown than a garment to sleep in. (Granville-Barker's note)

[13] The illustrator of the original volume.

[14] I do not know whether any archaeologically minded producer has yet substituted bagpipes. (Granville-Barker's note)

may; one can hardly say more. Here is a question of taste and matter for experiment. Certainly the horror of the scene for which Macbeth has left the chamber will be strengthened by a background of happy hospitality.[15] The contrast with the still ness to come and the fact that the scene which follows will call mainly for the same two actors in the same mood, should also be reckoned with. But it must be a distant background, no doubt.

Ho-boyes are noted again for the *Show of eight kings,* Banquo's descendants. And the recalling here by such unobtrusive means of Duncan's ceremonious welcome at Inverness would be valuable.

For Macbeth's kingship the Folio gives *A sennet sounded,* and no more.

But the drums, alarums, retreat and flourish of the battlefield must be considered. They are not meant to be mere noises. Just as the colours carried symbolised an army, so did these sounds symbolise upon that 'unrealistic' stage the varying phases of a battle. Treated as music they can be made symbolic; and though nowadays we have forgotten the alphabet of the convention, it is an easy one to re-learn. There is emotional value, too, in the sound of the trumpet. We need no learning to be stirred by that.

The Casting of the Parts

There will be the perennial difficulty of weighing the physical fitness or, it may be, the emotional power, of actors against their intellectual capacity. There can be no making of rules in the matter. To say that Macbeth must look like this or like that is to treat the play as a waxwork show. At the other extreme, to suppose that capacity to understand includes ability to express, is to confuse theatre with class-room. One may dogmatize a little upon temperament. One may – indeed one must – estimate the sheer, crude strength that a man needs to last out in the acting of such a part as Macbeth. One may sometimes say of any

---

[15] If he can be thought of as breaking suddenly away from the jovial company, unable to play his hypocritical part in it any longer, a much needed impetus is given to the soliloquy. (Granville-Barker's note)

part or of any passage: This *cannot* be so. The rest is immediate judgment.

It is interesting to recall that the actress most identified in public memory with Lady Macbeth sinned most, and perforce, against her own notion of the part. Mrs Siddons says she thought of the woman as 'fair, feminine, nay, perhaps even fragile.'[16] But – in her famous years at least – she played her like an avenging goddess. Without doubt she builded worse than she knew; and – this is the pity of it – the tradition of her superhuman presence has misguided many a performance since. Let us set aside the fact that Shakespeare had a boy of seventeen to play for him instead of a woman of forty, 'massive and concrete' – to quote a classic criticism of quite another performance[17] – and see simply what demands the text makes. The first is surely for swiftness of method. Macbeth at the outset is the hanger-back, his wife is the speeder on. She is the gadfly stinging him to action. He will not 'catch the nearest way'; the night's great business must be put into her 'despatch.' Such small hints, though, are nothing beside the sweep of purpose that informs her every line in these scenes; and the actress who plays them slowly yields her prime function in the play's action.[18] And swiftness will imply lightness of touch, though neither, needless to say, must connote hurry. There is certainly no textual evidence that Lady Macbeth was physically fragile. For obvious reasons a dramatist does not crib, cabin and confine the realization of his work in such a way.[19] But the dramatic gain in making her so is hardly disputable. The effect of the 'undaunted spirit' is doubled if we marvel that so frail a body

---

[16] Mrs Siddon's comments on Lady Macbeth are found in Thomas Campbell, *Life of Mrs Siddons*, London and New York, 1934, chapter VIII.

[17] Herbert and Pip's compliment to 'Mr Waldengarver's' performance of Hamlet, *Great Expectations*, chapter XXXI.

[18] Incidentally the play's balance will probably at once be upset, for no actor of good instinct will allow a performance to hang fire, and if the Lady Macbeth will not set a pace the Macbeth will be tempted to, much to the prejudice of his own character's development. (Granville-Barker's note)

[19] Shakespeare hardly ever marks down the physical appearance of his characters. In Falstaff, of course, he does. But, in a sense, Falstaff's bulk *is* his character. Maria in *Twelfth Night* is 'the youngest wren of nine.' But the repeated insistence upon her diminutiveness seems to denote a particular player. (Granville-Barker's note)

can contain it. There will be an appropriate beauty in her faint-
ing. A small matter this; but Shakespeare himself has touched in
the incident so sparely that if it is not rightly done on the very
stroke there is no dialogue or extra circumstance by which an
error can be retrieved. And the thin-drawn tragedy of her end
will be deepened.

We should see her even physically weighed down with the
crown and robes that she struck for. When

> Our hostess keeps her state,

it should seem as if the lonely, wan figure upon the throne had
no strength left to move. She does make one amazing effort to
save Macbeth from himself and from discovery.

> Are you a man? . . . O proper stuff!
> This is the very painting of your fear. . .
> Fie, for shame! . . .
> Think of this, good peers, but as a thing of custom . . .
> I pray you speak not; he grows worse and worse.

This is the old fire upflaring. But it exhausts her. When the two
are left alone she can say no more, do no more.

> You lack the season of all natures, sleep.

What an emptiness of hope and help underlies the phrase! He,
at heart as hopeless, responds with the bravado of

> Come, we'll to sleep.

Later it will be made very clear what sort of seasoning sleep
brings to her. And when next we see her in slumbery agitation
we should hardly be sure, but for the concern of the doctor and
her gentlewoman, whether this wraith that sighs and mutters
and drifts away is still a living creature or no.[20]

Then there is the commonplace but important consideration
of the contrast with Macbeth. About him there must be something colossal; and if this primary effect cannot be obtained by

---

[20] By nothing I say do I mean to imply that such a thing as the acting
of fragility is impossible. But Mrs Siddons – for an instance – apparently
found herself at too great a physical disadvantage in the matter, and aban-
doned all attempt to suggest it. (Granville-Barker's note)

direct means, every indirect resource must be used to suggest it. Not that mere physical bulk will avail. But Macbeth is a valiant man and, even before he becomes king, of an almost royal demeanour. He treats Duncan with a certain stiff dignity and Banquo with condescension. Only his wife knows the weakness that his high manner hides. And when he is king this demeanour is stamped even more deeply upon him. It has the greater effect because he keeps alone. Does he do so because he needs now to assert his will upon himself? Needs apart, he appears to find some satisfaction in exercising it on others. The length of the scene with Banquo's murderers has puzzled commentators. But is it not as if Macbeth, not content to give the fellows their orders and their pay, wanted to subdue their wills? One sees him pacing the floor and weaving words like spells round the two wretches, stopping every now and then to eye them hard and close. First he wants, above all, to commit them to a deeper guilt towards Banquo. This shows later in his cry of

> Thou canst not say I did it.

Duncan might justly fill his dreams. But Banquo was their enemy too, they hated him, they had done the deed: why then should he be haunted?

From the time we first see him as king, the figure of the man grows huger, harsher and gaunter. He loves his wife still. It is partly his very love that makes him keep himself from her; why should he damn her deeper with a share of the guilt to come?[21] Partly, no doubt, it is that he knows she is broken and useless. One of the few strokes of pathos that are let soften the grimness of the tragedy is Lady Macbeth's wan effort to get near enough to the tortured man to comfort him, But the royal robes, stiff on their bodies – stiff as with caked blood – seem to keep them apart. He has grown a stranger to her, who was once the

---

[21] Macbeth's views upon blood-guiltiness, however, were somewhat narrow, if our interpretation (above) of

> Thou canst not say I did it

may hold. He would then expect his wife to be whole-heartedly glad, for his sake, that Banquo was out of the way; it was enough for him to keep her in a most formal sense innocent of the knowledge for her to be able to applaud the deed with a clear conscience. (Granville-Barker's note)

inspiration of all he did![22] He treats her like a child:

> Be innocent of the knowledge, dearest chuck,
> Till thou applaud the deed.

Like an innocent child he cannot treat her. It is worth noting that, in this scene, Macbeth's mind is all upon the ill-powers of Nature – upon the powers that the weird sisters wield – as if it were their fellowship he now felt the need of.

We should mark, too, the bravery – and more than bravery – with which, later, he confronts the ghost. His nerves may give way, but he will not be the victim of his nerves. He dares it to come again, he drinks again to Banquo, his voice rises to the toast, clear, hearty, defiant. He means to test himself, to pit himself against every consequence of his deeds. 'Dare' is the note for all these passages. And, though he trembles still, it would seem that he wins; so to read,

> Hence, horrible shadow! Unreal mockery, hence!

and the ghost's vanishing.

Having outfaced this, he commits himself, from now on, to murder without scruple. And, as he loses humanity, he seems somehow to grow in physical strength. The power that went to make him man now goes to make him doubly brute, till, at the end, tied to a stake, he fights and dies like a wild beast indeed; and not till we see his severed head can we be sure that the evil life is out of him.

The actor of Macbeth has a mighty task. He must start at a pitch high enough to overtop his fellows; and the first part of the play will tax his judgment in balancing strength and weakness, conscience and ill ambition.[23] Between the

---

[22] To read

> But in them nature's copy's not eterne

as a suggestion of murder is quite wrong. From the point of view of the play's action a temptation to do what is already in the doing is weak. And this one line must then obscure the obvious meaning of every other line Lady Macbeth speaks in the scene. (Granville-Barker's note)

[23] For the foundations of Macbeth's character, and especially for a study of that power of conscienceless imagination that dominates it, one cannot do better than turn to the masterly *Shakespearean Tragedy* of A. C. Bradley. (Granville-Barker's note)

entrance as king and that line which looks to nethermost hell,

> We are yet but young in deed,

he has to carry his audience with him into such a world as Dante drew, where the spirit of man moves downward

> per l' aere amaro e sozzo.[24]

And in these scenes the technique of the play's writing, as it concerns the two chief characters, changes somewhat; and Shakespeare by his own great achievement adds to his interpreters' difficulties even while he offers them great chance of achievement too. For set the swift flow of the verse and the comparative directness and simplicity of the thoughts in the first part of the play beside this picture of the haunted desert of their souls, in which we are now to watch these two creatures moving, and note what a change of method is dictated to the actors for its realisation.

Macbeth's soliloquy in Act III, Scene i, and Lady Macbeth's four lines spoken alone in the following scene have clarity enough. But the rest of the dialogue is often but a mask behind which their minds are moving. Quite naturally, quite dramatically. Before they could talk freely to each other, these two. Now they cannot, and that in itself would begin their mutual tragedy. Sometimes the lines seem to carry echoes of a meaning which the speaker himself only dimly divines.

> It will have blood; they say blood will have blood;

and

> Strange things I have in head that will to hand,
> Which must be acted ere they may be scanned.

Here is more for the actor to do than to speak words, however expressively.

And, besides, there is all the unwritten motion of the play, the smiling menace to Banquo, the unspoken threat to the courtiers if they heed the 'strange inventions' that Malcolm and Donalbain are spreading abroad, the varied undercurrents dur-

---

[24] 'through foul and bitter air' (worse than that of Hell says the poet on the third terrace where anger is purged), *Purg.* XVI, 13.

ing the banquet scene. In all these attributes to the text the actor
must, so to speak, clothe himself; yet, be it ever remembered
that he must not *depreciate* the play's chief means of expression,
the winged words and the verse that charges them with
emotion.

From here to the play's end the part of Macbeth may be held
to suffer somewhat from Shakespeare's plan of it inevitably
lodging him in a dilemma. He means to brutalise the man, but
a man so brutalised becomes less capable of poetic expression.
The wild vigour with which the weird sisters are conjured comes
naturally enough. But later, is not Shakespeare apt to leap this
difficulty? Macbeth must moralise; so be it. But the sensibility
of

     I have liv'd long enough,

and

     I 'gin to be aweary of the sun,

does not go over well in close conjunction with

     I'll fight till from my bones my flesh be hack'd.

It is not that the inconsistency could not be explained away.
It is not even that there is in reality any inconsistency at all. It
is rather that, within the narrow limits of drama at least, a
character cannot be effectively developed in two directions at
once. Shakespeare is hurrying Macbeth, defiant to the last, towards a hopeless doom. It is true that this quick shifting of
mind in a man whose whole moral nature is in collapse, is a
recognisable thing. But, with so little more to do to the
character, Shakespeare has, for the sake of space perhaps, done
some of it rather arbitrarily; and these passages – beautiful as
they are, and, indeed, in their very beauty – are apt, straight-
forwardly interpreted, to seem to lie dead in the living body
of the rest. Either so, or they require such subtle rendering as in
itself is out of place.

When his wife is in question we do quite naturally catch the echo of Macbeth's earlier feelings for her, when he still could feel. The doctor tells him that she is

> . . . troubled with thick-coming fancies
> That keep her from her rest,

and his

> Cure her of that

comes, though hollowly, from his heart. But at once there follows the mocking

> Canst thou not minister to a mind diseased?

When he hears she is dead, by instinct he turns back silently to that earlier self to find his response. But there is none. He almost shrugs.

> She should have died hereafter.

Then, perhaps, he might have felt something, found some meaning in her loss. But now his only relief is to burst into a rage of pessimism. Whatever meaning has this life at all?

> It is a tale
> Told by an idiot, full of sound and fury,
> Signifying nothing.

It will be safe to suggest to most actors that in this last section of the play they should set themselves above all to avoid sententiousness. Macbeth sententious!

With regard to Banquo one can hardly do better than – with the thanks due for this as for so much else in the study of Shakespeare – quote Professor Bradley's analysis of his character.

'. . . Banquo is evidently a bold man, probably an ambitious one, and certainly has no lurking guilt in his ambition.'

'. . . he would repel the "cursed thoughts" [that the weird sisters had prompted in him]; and they are mere thoughts, not intentions. But still they are "thoughts," something more, probably, than mere recollections; and they bring with them an undefined sense of guilt. The poison has begun to work. [After the murder] . . . we may be pretty sure that he suspects the truth at once . . . He is profoundly shocked, full of indignation, and determined to play the part of a brave and honest man.

'But he plays no such part. When next we see him, on the last day of his life, we find that he has yielded to evil. The witches and his own ambition have conquered him. He alone of the lords knew of the prophecies, but he has said nothing of them. He has acquiesced in Macbeth's accession, and in the official theory that Duncan's sons had suborned the chamberlains to murder him. . . . He has, not formally but in effect, "cloven to" Macbeth's "consent"; he is knit to him by "a most indissoluble tie". . . . And his soliloquy tells us why:

> Thou hast it now : King, Cawdor, Glamis, all,
> As the weird women promised, and, I fear,
> Thou play'dst most foully for't : yet it was said
> It should not stand in thy posterity,
> But that myself should be the root and father
> Of many kings. If there come truth from them—
> As upon thee, Macbeth, their speeches shine –
> Why, by the verities on thee made good
> May they not be my oracles as well,
> And set me up in hope? But hush! no more.

This "hush! no more" is not the dismissal of "cursed thoughts": it only means that he hears the trumpets announcing the entrance of the King and Queen. His punishment comes swiftly, much more swiftly than Macbeth's, and saves him from any further fall.'

What better guidance could producer or actor ask?

The occasion of Macduff's introduction to the play should be noted. He appears in Duncan's train at Inverness, but does not speak. The discovery of the murder, however, is given to him. And it is obvious that Shakespeare requires a voice to ring out clear, candid and unafraid with

> O horror! horror! horror! Tongue nor heart
> Cannot conceive nor name thee!

His voice should be like light breaking in – even though it be a stormy sunrise. This extreme contrast with what has gone before is a very necessary effect. And candour is Macduff's keynote. He is placed in direct contrast to Macbeth; he stands, moreover, in blunt relief against the other tactful courtiers. Shakespeare is sparing of material in this play, but here is enough, and it can be given point to. The immediate

> Wherefore did you so?

when Macbeth lets out that he has killed the grooms, followed by observant silence, is worth, well acted and well arranged, a dozen expository speeches. By his retort to the pliant Rosse's

> Will you to Scone?
> No, cousin, I'll to Fife,

any sufficient actor can so fix the character and its dramatic purpose in our memory that his re-appearance even after many scenes will have full importance.

The scene in England needs as careful handling as any in the play and is commonly held not to repay the care; most producers hack at its text mercilessly. But this – principles apart – is penny-wise policy. The scene is the starting-point of the play's counter-action, and everything should be done to enhance its importance. Malcolm is to be king of Scotland. He is thought by most actors an ungrateful part, but Shakespeare at least did not leave him a nonentity. It will be useful to enquire why this scene is, as it is, a long level of verse, with its thoughts and emotions, till toward the end, rather catalogued than spontaneously springing. One simple explanation is that at this point in the play's writing Shakespeare was tired – as well he might be, after what had come before – but had to push on somehow. And we know that he all but transcribed a considerable passage from Holinshed. In the result the scene has been accounted dull – as dull, the irreverent might protest, as the virtue it chronicles. But we must look carefully to the playwright's intention. He needed for his audience, if not for himself, a breathing-space in which to recover from the shaking effects of the tragedy as he had so far developed it, and to prepare for the final rush of events. For this purpose a short scene would not suffice. He had already provided in the scene between Rosse, the old man and Macduff, and in the scene between Lenox and another lord, intervals of calm contrast with the bloody business of the play's main action. And it is, incidentally, most important to give these scenes their full value, to let the music of their smoother

verse bring some relief to our ear, and the irony of their
content – for the contrast is not a violent one – set our
thoughts to work after our emotion has been so played upon.

But now neither would an unemotional scene suffice. Most
certainly Scotland is not to be saved by the like of the cool time-
serving Rosse and Lenox. They may be well-intentioned men
enough. But Macduff marks even their greatest worth at such
a time (and Malcolm's, as he thinks) with

> Great tyranny, lay thou thy basis sure,
> For goodness dares not check thee!

That Malcolm might be what his self-accusation would make
him, that Macduff might be Macbeth's spy, that each then
should turn from the other in loathing, and that Macduff should
not be too easily convinced of the truth – all this is necessary as
a solid foundation for the moral dominance of the rest of the
play by these two. And the whole matter must be given space
and weight to the measure of its importance. There is a formalism in the writing, true; and it may be more formal than
Shakespeare could and would have made it at a more favourable
moment. But even in the formalism there is significance.
Malcolm is meant to be a young man who is deliberately
virtuous, level-headed moreover, and astute. And however un-
heroic such a figure may seem to the romantically-minded play-
goer, Shakespeare will have it that this is the man to save
Scotland. Given an actor of the right authority for Malcolm,
the scene can be made interesting enough. A thing in it to make
clear and stress carefully is the opposition between the natures
of the two men and their ways of approach to each other: Macduff outspoken; Malcolm reserved, over-cautious at first, though
never cold. From its beginning, indeed, the scene is, beneath the
surface, well charged with emotion. And Macduff's line,

> Such welcome and unwelcome things at once
> 'Tis hard to reconcile,

which one has often heard an actor speak with an air of tame
puzzlement, is really the passionate, half-choked utterance of a
man still torn between hope and despair.

We have before noted the value of the little interlude
of the doctor's entrance and the speech about the King's

Evil. And the rest of the scene is plain sailing.[25]

Rosse must be carefully cast. It is a 'stock-company' tradition that this part was the last insult that could be offered to a responsible actor. On the other hand pages have been written by an ingenious gentleman to demonstrate that he is the motive force and the real villain of the play.[26] To bring this home in performance, he would, one fears, have to be accompanied throughout by an explanatory chorus. But he is, in truth, a not uninteresting figure. The part is threaded more consecutively through the play than any other. Confronted with each catastrophe, Rosse stands emotionally untouched. He stands, indeed, as a kind of silent or smoothly speaking and cynical chorus to the tragic happenings. With great matter in hand, Shakespeare is, as we have noticed, thrifty in the writing of his minor parts; in this play thriftier perhaps than in any other. Unless, therefore, the producer so wills and most carefully contrives, nothing much can be made of the part. It is a negative figure. But that is its significance, and a most valuable one. And with care and intelligent acting this 'ever-gentle' gentleman, with his

> Alas, the day,

his

> Gentlemen, rise, his highness is not well,

his

> You must have patience, madam,

his admirable tact when he brings the news to Macduff of his children's and wife's slaughter, his smooth sympathy with Siward for his son's death, may be made very distinctive.[27] He

---

[25] May I register an opinion, though, that it is *Malcolm's* eye in Scotland that would create soldiers, and that it is Macbeth who is referred to as having no children. There is no proving this. But the implication that Macduff is there turning to Rosse for comfort is an unnatural one. (Granville-Barker's note)

[26] M. F. Libby, *Some New Notes on Macbeth*, Toronto, 1893 (cited in the revised *Variorum* edition, ed. H. H. Furness, Jr., Philadelphia, 1903.)

[27] He is silent at the discovery of Duncan's murder, and modern editions even omit to mark his entrance, which F1 gives with Macbeth and Lenox; but his silent presence can be made most effective. Or is the direction evidence of a mere stage-manager's anxiety to augment his crowd, and did Shakespeare's Rosse think it more politic to stay in bed when he heard the alarm bell? (Granville-Barker's note)

is more of a 'Renaissance' figure than the others. He is, in the old sense of the word, a politician. He is the play's taciturn *raisonneur*.

The part of Lady Macduff is in itself very easily effective; the child's part, mettlesomely played, even more so. The only trouble with the scene can be that it is too effective; within three or four minutes, that is to say, a direful catastrophe is precipitated upon two characters with whom we are hardly acquainted, and without, therefore, sufficient aesthetic cause. Shakespeare helps us over this difficulty by giving scope for a well-coloured, positive personality; and this should determine a Lady Macduff's casting. With her first line she can make herself sufficiently known to the audience:

What had he done to make him fly the land?

It is important, too, that the killing of the child should be done very deliberately. The thing is so abhorrent that we are apt to try and gloss it over in action. This is a mistake. The dramatic enormity is belittled by the open-eyed, heroic readiness with which the child faces death. This heroism strikes the note upon which the scene must end.

To pass upon some details. There is a tradition – one of those quite unreliable stage traditions – which speaks of the porter as the Drunken Porter, and makes him in appearance a candidate for an inebriates' home. For such a painful effort at comedy Shakespeare gives us no warrant. Truly the porter had been carousing till the second cock, and no doubt the news of the victory and the king's visit made it a good occasion for getting drunk. But he answers Macduff's joke about it quite aptly, and his delay in opening the gates can presumably be accounted for by his unwilling waking, the getting on of clothes and boots, and the finding a light for his lantern. Drunk on this occasion and on others he may have been, but it does not prove him a confirmed sot.

Banquo's murderers are commonly made ruffians fetched from the gutter. But the text's implication is surely that they were officers, cast perhaps for some misdemeanour and out of luck. Certainly the lovely lines,

> The west yet glimmers with some sreaks of day.
> Now spurs the lated traveller apace
> To gain the timely inn,

are not gutter-bred, and Macbeth's speech to them, beginning,

> Ay, in the catalogue ye go for men,

loses half its point if they are not men come down in the world.
The third murderer is obviously a private and particular spy of
Macbeth's, and his unheralded appearance (like that of the
fellow who warns Lady Macduff of her danger) is in itself
significant enough, significant too of the whole state of Macbeth's kingdom, with its spies, and spies upon spies; when, as
Rosse says,

> . . . we hold rumour
> From what we fear, yet know not what we fear.

We must note, too, the masterly effect produced when these
three stand with Banquo's body at their feet, the light out, and
the stillness around – which they but half break with their curt
whispering.

It is important that the doctor and the waiting gentlewoman
should not – as the stage phrase goes – try to play Lady
Macbeth's part for her in the sleep-walking scene. He is intent
on his case, she mainly obsessed with a queen's waiting-
woman's anxiety to hush up the scandal. Beside Lady Macbeth
herself they must seem pettifogging, or she cannot show tragic
to the full. The doctor has his couplet too, when Macbeth has
flung off the stage in berserk rage:

> Were I from Dunsinane away and clear,
> Profit again should hardly draw me here.

This has been condemned as un-Shakespearean and beneath the
dignity of the tragedy. But when Shakespeare saw a chance to
salt the meat of his plays with such touches he did not stand
upon tragic dignity. He had enough of that to spare and to
waste upon us whenever he chose.

Duncan can hardly be misread. He is often made older than
need be, and sometimes too consistently meek and usually too
lachrymose. There are actors with an unhappy knack of taking

one point in a part – and a minor one – as a peg upon which
to hang the whole. And Duncan's 'plenteous joys' seeking to
hide themselves in 'drops of sorrow' are apt to be used to water
the character down to an undue depression; and with this will
sag the play's whole beginning, one aspect of which the king's
figure must dominate. His arrival at Inverness should be, in a
simple way, as stately as possible. His lines here have fine turns
of thought and feeling, and a most royal ring about them.
And

> By your leave, hostess,

seems to indicate that, as the custom was, he kisses Lady
Macbeth's cheek. What better climax and ending could the
scene have?

The problem of presenting the weird sisters is more deeply
rooted than in any corruption of the text. We can cut away most
of Middleton with confidence, and quite banish his creatures of
comic opera from our minds, and the remainder may be true
Shakespeare; but what the positive embodiment of Shakespeare's
conception should be this simple sum in subtraction by no
means leaves clear. That he himself calls them weird sisters and
not (proveably) witches is something, and might lead us straight
to Holinshed's 'three women in strange and wild apparel,
resembling creatures of elder world,' if it were not that both
Holinshed in another passage and Shakespeare's own writing
of the later scene give equal colour to a more commonplace
conception. This part of Act IV, Scene i, is intrinsically more
Shakespearean than the earlier scenes in which the witches
appear without Macbeth – though, truly, it is a weakness in
criticism to be always maintaining that what is well done is by
Shakespeare and what is ill done is by somebody else. This,
however, is the more likely to be Shakespeare in that Holinshed's
creatures for this particular purpose are 'certaine wizards' and 'a
certaine witch.'[28] Yet Macbeth says that he will to the 'weird
sisters.' It seems pretty clear that Shakespeare deliberately

---

[28] True, Shakespeare might have disregarded Holinshed here and Middleton, by a coincidence, have adhered to him. By coincidence, because he
would hardly have deliberately rejected Shakespeare and yet sought Shakespeare's source. (Granville-Barker's note)

blended the two types. In the composite as we have it there is risk in claiming too much emphasis for the first. He may have continued to call them the weird sisters only because he had begun by calling them so. On the other hand, the part of their witchcraft that is essential to the play is given dignity and mystery, and it may be – it *may* be – that their incantations round the cauldron, which are given strength and good colour but no more, are, in form at least, Middleton's after all.

When it comes to their presentation on the stage one may perhaps proceed usefully by negation. Though they have supernatural powers, they are *not* supernatural beings. They are *not*, on the other hand, the sort of old women that Shakespeare may have seen ducked in the horse-pond at Stratford. And if his superstitious fancies on those occasions glorified such poor wretches somewhat, we should still be bound for stage purposes to consider a little what our fancies would confer on the same figures.

If we look, where we should usually look for a description, to the impression made upon some opposite character, to whom it is given to interpret an unusual figure to the audience, we find:

> . . . What are these
> So wither'd and so wild in their attire,
> That look not like th' inhabitants o' the earth
> And yet are on't?

and again:

> How now, you secret, black, and midnight hags!

And that surely paints them for us with sufficient clarity.

The last part of the play calls for the producer's very firm control of the elements that may otherwise, so to speak, run away with it. It is notable – though in the play's staging as a rule too little noticed – with what a very strong hand Shakespeare himself has controlled them. One need not again inveigh against the senseless omission from most productions of such a scene as that in which the revolted Scottish lords gather together, nor against the telescoping of those that picture Malcolm's advance. This misconduct alone tends to pile up the other part of the action into a lurid chaos and to make the strain on any player of Macbeth unbearable. But, right to the end, Shakespeare has most carefully balanced the horrible by the heroic. Young Siward's death and his father's fortitude is set against Macbeth's slaughtering and the uplifting of his severed head. And to wallow in the horror and omit the beauty and dignity is to degrade great tragedy to the depth of poor melodrama.

In character development Shakespeare has perhaps done all he can do – for his protagonists at least – even before the end of Act III. The rest is catastrophe, skilfully retarded. But in his marshalling of the play's action to its end, he surely outdoes even his own accustomed mastery in such matters. We have, in the scene with the weird sisters, the whipping up of the evil in Macbeth to the top of its fury, immediately followed by its most savage outbreak – sudden and short – upon Lady Macduff and the child. Then comes, as we have remarked, the elaborate and weighty preparation for the play's counter-action; an outspoken scene. In contrast to this follows the scene of sickness and whisperings and unnatural troubles, the scene of the slow perishing of one of the two evil beings of the play. Quickly after comes the gathering of the Scottish lords, like men escaping from prison and despair. The 'drum and colours' here strike a new note; lifted spirits are marked by such means as the rising inflection of Angus's second speech with its 'Now . . . Now . . . Now . . .'; and the repeated 'March we on' and 'Make we our march' begins the movement to the play's end.

Macbeth himself is, so to say, the fixed point towards which this movement sweeps. We are to see him at intervals, waiting the approach and desperate at having to wait, for this, as we know, was not his sort of soldiership. In the first of these scenes of his we have talk of preparation, but Shakespeare allows it none of the cheerful panoply of war, neither 'drum' nor 'colours.' Instead there is depression and distraction, the news of the flying of the Thanes, the terror of the 'cream-faced loon,' and, to clinch the effect, Macbeth's own contrariness about his armour – one of those simple touches that help to throw great issues into relief.

The following scene is so short that it is possible to give it the effect of an unhalting march. The Scottish and English armies are joined, their number is doubled. Malcolm has the leadership. But the last two voices are Macduff's and Siward's – to whom a very ringing speech is given, emphasis of his dignity and importance as the English general.

Now on Macbeth's side the martial note is sounded, and sounded loudly. This scene is more rhythmically written than his earlier one, and is meant to be more rapid. It has but two checks to its pace, the news of the Queen's death, and the couplet,

> I 'gin to be aweary of the sun;

and the latter may be designed to emphasise by contrast the rush of the end. The bringing of the news of the moving wood immediately upon the first reflective moment indicates an even greater contrast. At this point, if one were charting the scene as a fever is charted, one would show a perpendicular leap in energy. And the mere vocal effect of the passage beginning,

> Arm, arm, and out,

should be in itself an alarum bell.

Then follows, again, an interesting check and contrast. Malcolm's army is before Dunsinane, at rest for a moment. He and Siward coolly plan their battle. The trumpet-toned couplet at the end is given, for obvious reasons, to Macduff.

The actual conduct of the last scene upon Shakespeare's stage we have already discussed. Its inward scheme is not hard to determine, though, with so much movement involved, it may not be too easy to abide by in practice. It divides, dramatically, into three parts. The first runs to Macduff's discovery of Macbeth with

> Turn, hell-hound, turn.

This goes, as we say, ding-dong, and any possible half-pauses are filled up with 'alarums.' Macbeth is grim and deadly, a trapped beast; his comings and goings have no purpose in them. Moreover, as the battle goes forward he becomes conscious that his mind too has been trapped and tricked, though he cannot yet see how. He is invulnerable; again and again he returns to this. But, as certainly, with the battle against him, he is doomed. Is the answer to the riddle that he must kill himself? Must he 'play the Roman fool'? He fights, one would suppose, like an automaton and perhaps the more dangerously for that.

In clear contrast is the gallant, crusading figure of young Siward, flashing to his death.

There is none of the glow of battle upon Macduff. Methodically, determinedly, he pursues his single purpose. For a relief we have the interlude when the two generals, cool and confident still, enter the castle.

The second part concerns Macbeth and Macduff alone. Nice critics have found Macbeth's last fling of words — beloved of every schoolboy — too highly flavoured with bombast. They may be. But Shakespeare, having brought his play to the issue of sheer physical combat, might well think it appropriate to throw niceness behind him.[29] This is to be a mortal combat and a mighty combat. For Macduff to come easily by his vengeance would be unsatisfying. For Macbeth to go easily out would be incredible, and to give him a finely worded end might seem to redeem him, if ever so little. This Shakespeare will not do. He allows him one gleam of incorrigible pride, he leaves him his animal courage. For the rest, he sends him shouting to hell. And from the beginning the exchange of speeches between the two men should be like the exchange of blows.

The end of the play is contrived as a full and varied orchestra of voices with the trumpets of victory topping them. Malcolm and his soldiers enter processionally, and at once we are given the suggestion of order restored. The note of pity for the dead is struck, and upon it comes the practised soldier's stoic response. There is Rosse's smooth sympathy. There is the defiant nobility with which Siward takes his own son's death; and for Malcolm there is a needed touch of impulsive generosity.

Macduff's entrance, lifting the severed head, changes the key almost violently. Here is an echo of the now ended tragedy. Vengeance is accomplished, but Macduff, widowed and childless, stands apart from all thoughtless rejoicing.

---

[29] Not that he ever took much stock in it. (Granville-Barker's note)

I see thee compassed with thy kingdom's pearl.

But he is a man alone. His voice must have the music of a selfless and unforgettable sorrow in it.

Then, with the careful modulation of Malcolm's address to his people, Shakespeare brings us at his ease back to our work-a-day world.

Textual Variants

THE references are to the Arden edition – the *Macbeth* volume being edited by Henry Cuningham, – which is taken as a standard text.[30]

In general: omit all scene description. The scene division itself is sometimes quite arbitrary.

Act i, Scene i.	Spurious.
Scene ii.	For some remarks upon its general validity, see the body of this Preface.
21.	Cut 'which ne'er shook hands.' This at least will relieve the actor from talking nonsense.
45.	'*Enter Rosse.*' Restore '*and Angus*' from F1.
Scene iii.	Omit 1-36. For reasons, see body of the Preface.
68-9.	To be spoken by all three sisters, agreeably to Mr Cuningham's footnote. Incidentally, this is the theatrical tradition.
Scene vi.	For 'proposes' read 'purposes.' This is presumably a misprint in the Arden edition itself.
Act ii, Scene i.	'*Enter Banquo,*' etc. 'Take thee that too'

---

[30] Nor should I forget to record the great use that Mr Cuningham's own notes have been to me, and my thanks for them. (Granville-Barker's note)

seems to imply that Banquo was carrying the torch, and had, besides Fleance, no torch-bearer with him. He could not conveniently carry the torch during the dialogue with Macbeth.

Scene iii, 92. *'Re-enter Macbeth and Lenox.'* Add *'and Rosse.'* This restoration of the F1 direction is important.

Act III, Sc. ii, 121. 'But wail his fall.' The 'But' is surely corrupt, and possibly the rest of the passage too. 'would' — see footnote — makes it a little better.

Scene iv, 74 & 107. *'Exit ghost'* after *'Enter ghost'* is quite adequate as a direction.

102. Put semicolon after 'blood,' and omit it after 'say.'

Scene v. Spurious.

Act IV, Sc. i, 39-47. Omit.

97. Read 'rebellion's head.'

124. Omit 'What! is this so?'

125-132. Omit. Direction to read *'Exeunt witches.'*

153-155. A good case can be made for the omission of 'No boasting . . . sights.' Its sense is pure repetition of 'From this moment . . . hand,' which comes but four lines earlier, and it smells strongly of Middleton.

Scene ii, 38-59. For retention *versus* omission, see the body of this Preface.

Act IV, Sc. iii, 236. 'God, God,' in place of 'Heaven,' if one might follow that authoritative emendation, would be a great strengthening.

Act v, Scene i, 35. Certainly, as the footnote claims, the punctuation of F1, with the full stop.

Scene v, 42. Read 'pall' for 'pull.'

'Preface' to THE TRAGEDIE OF MACBETH, London, Ernest Benn Ltd., 1923, pp. xxv–lix. (The first volume of *The Players' Shakespeare*.)

NOTE: In a letter to Harcourt Williams, January 25, 1930, Granville-Barker says this 'Preface' is 'full of blunders' (quoted in C. B. Purdom, *Harley Granville Barker: Man of the Theatre, Dramatist and Scholar*, London: Rockliff Publishing Corp. Ltd., 1955, p. 234). See also the letter to Sir John Gielgud, October 27, 1940, printed *Ibid.*, p. 267.